• HALSGROVE DISCOVER SERIES ➤

ANCIENT PEAKLAND

• HALSGROVE DISCOVER SERIES ➤

ANCIENT PEAKLAND

BILL BEVAN

HALSGROVE

First published in Great Britain in 2007

Disclaimer
While the author has walked all the routes described in the book, no responsibility can be
accepted for any omissions or errors or for any future changes that may occur in the details given.
The author and publisher cannot accept any liability for accident, mishap,
or loss arising from the use of this book.

British Library Cataloguing-in-Publication Data
A CIP record for this title is available from the British Library

ISBN 978 1 84114 593 8

HALSGROVE
Halsgrove House, Ryelands Farm Industrial Estate,
Bagley Green, Wellington, Somerset TA21 9PZ
Tel: 01823 653777   Fax: 01823 216796
email: sales@halsgrove.com
website: www.halsgrove.com

Printed and bound by D'Auria Industrie Grafiche, Italy

Contents

Acknowledgements

Thank you to Roly Smith for first asking me to write a guide book to the Peak District's accessible ancient archaeological monuments. I also thank Ken Smith, John Barnatt and Mark Edmonds for sharing many stimulating conversations and ideas about what these many sites tell us about past societies. Thank you also to those I dragged out to visit many of the places in this book.

The following photographs are not mine but have been provided by a number of organisations and individuals for which I am extremely grateful. They are all copyright of the respective named organisations and individuals.

Robert Nicholls, Paleocreations, kindly supplied his reconstructions of Cresswell Crags: page 10 left, page 21 left, page 21 right, page 23 top and page 24 left.

Cresswell Heritage Trust also provided the following photographs: page 5 and page 22 left, page 17, page 23 bottom, and page 24 right.

Steve Fox drew the following for the Peak District National Park Authority: page 58, page 88 bottom right, page 88 top right, page 88 left, page 91 and page 127 bottom for Poole's Cavern.

Gary Short drew page 38 and page 50 top left for the Peak District National Park Authority.

Mellor Archaeological Trust/Greater Manchester Archaeological Unit provided page 19, page 106 and page 107.
Sheffield Galleries & Museums Trust page 28, page 36, page 63 bottom, and page 133.
Poole's Cavern page 33, page 35 bottom, page 112, page 113 bottom, page 127 top and page 128.

Page 63 top, page 59, page 89, page 99, page 90, page 98, page 100, page 110, page 111, page 131, and page 134 top left, are all courtesy of the Peak District National Park Authority's Cultural Heritage Team photographic collection.

Page 92, page 101 and page 119 are courtesy of the English Heritage National Monument Record, Swindon.

Nine Stone Close was built about 4000 years ago as a place for ceremonies.

Introduction

A*ncient Peakland* is written to encourage you to go out and discover many of the impressive monuments and buildings that survive from over 9000 years of the Peak District's past. We begin with the thawing of northern Europe at the end of the last Ice Age about 10,000 years ago and end with the Norman Conquest of 1066.

Many impressive prehistoric, Romano-British and early medieval monuments were built during this long time span. Some survive in those odd corners of fields which have not been put to the plough; others have lain undisturbed on remote moorlands. Beautiful carved artwork can be found in churchyards. Like the pages of a novel left outside, some of its words smudged by the rain, a few pages torn by the wind, all of these sites have stories to tell about the people who built them. People who lived and died here, who tended farms and gathered to worship many different gods. This they did on ground you can still walk over today. In places you can follow almost in their exact footsteps by walking through entrances and the locations of doorways, some of which are three or even four thousand years old.

This book will guide you to those time-drenched odd corners and help you to read the weathered texts. Of course, these 'words' are not real words written down in ancient scripts. There are precious few written words to describe life in the Peak District before the Domesday Book of the first Norman king. A record of William the Conqueror's new acquisition, tabulated to list and valuate lands he had taken by force, Domesday was compiled in 1086. The Peak District barely raises a couple of sentences before this date. A Roman word stamped on lead ingots and an entry in a Saxon tax document are about all. Without writing, what we know of the Peak District comes from archaeology, from the lumps under the grass and architectural

Archaeologists excavate an early Iron Age site surviving below the peat of Gardom's Edge on the Peak District moorlands.

Ornate stone crosses carved over 1000 years ago survive in many church-yards, most moved there from their original positions.

The Peak District would have looked like this scene from Cresswell Crags about 12,000 years ago.

fragments. There are Ice Age cave shelters, including the famous Cresswell Crags. After the ice thawed, successive generations built burial mounds, henges stone circles, fields and timber houses during the 8000 years of later Prehistory. The Romans brought forts with them a little under 2000 years ago to control the important lead veins and farmers cultivated fields under Imperial rule. Britons, Saxons and Vikings settled in the region after the Romans left, burying their dead in mounds and erecting ornately carved crosses to the new religion from the East. This multicultural mix was what the Normans found here when their barons took control and brought Domesday with them.

There were great changes in human society during this long time period. Nearly 2000 generations have been born and died during this vast time period if we take each generation to be twenty-five years, the average age of parents when children are born. Somebody born in 2007 might only be 20 generations away from their direct ancestors born 500 years earlier in 1507. This is a very long time indeed with grandparents multiplied by 2000 stretching back way into the distant, distant past!

Dales and narrow valleys such as the Manifold are typical of the limestone.

The Peak District is an upland region of contrasts. At its heart is the rolling limestone plateau, which is dissected by steep dales and narrow gorges. Grey white limestone walls give the plateau its characteristic look. Most were built within the last 250 years, their ruler-straight lines enclosing open commons into regular shaped fields of improved pasture. The limestone is surrounded by a horseshoe of gritstone moorlands. These rise to a height of 500 metres above sea level in the north where they form the southern end of the Pennines, the spine of England that runs north to meet the Cheviots in Northumberland. Covered in a blanket of peat, the moorlands are dominated by heather that is alive with radiant purple flowers in late summer. Wide valleys separate the gritstone and limestone. The longest is the wooded Derwent. It collects amongst the High Peak peat and flows south past Matlock and Derby to join the River Trent. The Derwent's eastern side is flanked by the Eastern Edges, sheer rock gritstone cliffs such as Stanage, Froggatt and Gardom's.

The wide sweep of Dovedale gently cuts through the Peak District's limestone country.

The limestone plateau is divided by regular grids of grey white dry-stone walls.

The dramatic gritstone moorlands surrounding the limestone plateau glow purple with summer flowering heather.

The wide Derwent Valley has been flooded to create reservoirs near its moorland source.

Beds of gritstone lain down one on top of each other over 300 million years ago.

Popular with climbers, Stanage Edge is one of many gritstone cliffs that rise above the Derwent Valley.

The limestone plateau from Mam Tor hillfort. Ancient monuments and archaeological sites survive where later farming has not swept them away.

The moorlands have been little touched since prehistory, preserving many archaeological sites and monuments.

The Peak District is rich in ancient sites because of these uplands. There are many places that have just not been suitable for cereal cultivation since the medieval period, some that have not been intensively farmed from Prehistory. On the limestone plateau, most of the archaeological sites survive on patches of thin soils, on high ridges or in steep-sided dales. We are fortunate that the Romano-British village of Chee Tor survives because of the decisions made by those who settled there to choose a rocky promontory. It is on the edge of a medieval common field belonging to Blackwell village. Medieval ploughing within intensively cultivated common fields has obliterated an unknown number of ancient sites across the limestone and the larger valleys. The common fields were surrounded by grassland pastures for sheep and cattle and the ground was left relatively undisturbed. Chee Tor and some of its fields perched on a steep daleside are separated by the featureless flat ground of the common field. Many prehistoric burial mounds survive on the limestone thanks to the choices made to bury the dead on high hilltops and prominent ridges that have been beyond the reach of most farmers since. Vast Prehistoric landscapes of fields and the faint traces of houses exist on the gritstone moorlands. These, and probably all of the suitable land in the Peak District, were settled and farmed for upwards of 1000 years until just before the Roman invasion. They survived because the moorlands became marginal to more recent agriculture.

Antiquarian Adventures and the Barrow Knight

The wealth of visible earthworks and monuments in the Peak District first attracted the attention of antiquarians keen to order a labourer to put spade to turf in the eighteenth century. Two of the first were a reverend and a major. These were gentlemen with a little learning, time on their hands and enough of an income to fund their interests. The Reverend Evatt excavated a barrow at Wardlow in the 1760s. Major Rooke, a Fellow of the Society of Antiquaries, did the same to barrows on Stanton Moor in the 1780s. They were the home-staying explorers of their time, describing the antiquities of regions in terms reminiscent of those searching for the North-West Passage or Timbuctoo. Stanton Moor was the most popular destination with other gentlemen and reverends retrieving funerary urns from barrows – usually referred to as tumuli – in subsequent decades.

Early excavations at Cresswell Crags.

The Peak District waited another generation for its most famous and prolific antiquarian to take the field. Thomas Bateman was born in Rowsley, Derbyshire on the 8th November 1821 to a moderately wealthy local land-owning family. His father, William, was himself a keen antiquarian but died in 1835 and Thomas moved to Middleton Hall to be raised by his grandfather. He became interested in archaeology while helping to run the family estate and after reading antiquarian accounts of excavations in Wiltshire. Bateman decided that digging barrows was how he would spend much of his time and family income. When he started, he didn't hang around. He excavated thirty-eight barrows in 1845. Two years later he published the results of his and earlier antiquarians' work in *Vestiges of the Antiquities of Derbyshire*. Bateman worked through another fifty barrows in 1848 and 1849 but became ill in 1850 and only managed another twenty-two excavations between 1851 and his death in 1861. He published his second book, *Ten Years' Diggings in Celtic and Saxon Grave Hills in the Counties of Derby, Stafford and York* the year he died. Both are classics of Victorian archaeology in the Peak District and are still referred to today by archaeologists studying the region's prehistoric monuments. The sheer extent of Bateman's work earned him the nickname of the Barrow Knight. He built up a large museum of his own finds in his home, Lomberdale Hall, but his son later sold most of the collection. Some artefacts were acquired by Buxton Museum and Weston Park Museum in Sheffield.

Antiquarian excavations at Arbor Low employed labourers, children and ponies.

Bateman's baton was taken up by his main accomplice – Samuel Carrington. Carrington was twenty-three years older than Bateman, a schoolmaster from Wetton, Staffordshire. He had directly supervised many barrow excavations for Bateman after Bateman's ill health as well as digging his own sites in Staffordshire. Carrington is perhaps most memorable for excavating the long barrow on the aptly named Long Low near Alstonefield. He also conducted one of the earliest excavations of a Romano-British rural – or 'native' – settlement when he explored buildings close to his home in Wetton between 1845 and 1852. He enthusiastically described the settlement as the 'Pompeii of the North' and mused that a flat stone scratched with regular marks was presumably the result of idle time without Sunday papers.

Many more excavations have followed these pioneers of Peak District archaeology, each in turn adding to our knowledge. The standards of recording common in the days of Bateman and Carrington were significantly lower than those accepted by today's archaeologists. Locations of sites and their contents were described in somewhat vague terms. Archaeologists trying to reconstruct Bateman's discoveries may sometimes be found walking lost across a Peak District field or moor while trying to follow his directions to a barrow given in relation to a nearby hill top or field wall. Today, excavations are usually only carried out if there is some risk to a monument, usually from erosion as at Nine Ladies, or if there is an important research question that needs answering. One of the most recent major archaeological projects was on Gardom's Edge, a moorland landscape packed full of the

Volunteers stand in the impressive enclosure ditch at Mellor.

19

remains of prehistoric houses, fields and enclosures. Excavations were carried out between 1995 and 2000 to assess what survives below ground, to research the nature of settlement and farming and to tell a wide audience about life on the Peak District's Eastern Moors over 2000 years ago. Thousands of visitors made the journey across the moorland to see the latest discoveries. A similar project has been digging under lawns and fields at the Old Vicarage in Mellor ever since the occupants spotted a suspicious line of parched grass one dry summer. The Greater Manchester Archaeological Unit and Mellor Archaeological Trust have unearthed evidence for an important Iron Age and Romano-British settlement enclosed within a massive ditch. Both Gardom's and Mellor have enabled large numbers of people to participate in making vital discoveries about their local ancient heritage.

Accessible Time Travel

The Peak District is a very accessible destination to visit ancient sites and monuments. All of the sites to visit in this guide are on public rights of way or open access land. Most are convenient to visitor accommodation, public transport routes or car parks; some involve a long walk across open moorland or through fields. This is pointed out under the entry for each site, along with a grid reference. The Ordnance Survey Explorer Maps, OL1 and OL24 (Dark Peak and White Peak), are good companions to help you explore all of the sites.

The creation of the Peak District National Park in 1951 has done much to benefit those ancient monuments lying within the Park boundary. The National Park has an obligation to work with landowners to help conserve them and make them accessible to the public where possible. Many more stone circles and barrows, as well as Arbor Low, can now be reached along rights of way or are explained by visitor boards than was the case over fifty years ago.

CHAPTER 1
Ice Age Hunters

As a prelude to the region's history it is worth going back further in time. During the last Ice Age, between 50,000 and 10,000 years ago, the Peak District lay at the edge of the mighty glaciers that reached south from the Arctic. These glaciers were several kilometres thick and covered much of the northern hemisphere. Beyond them lay a vast expanse of permanently frozen land similar to the tundra of Siberia today. Small bands of people travelled across the tundra. They lived in caves and temporary shelters, hunting and foraging for their food, surrounded by animals such as woolly mammoths, woolly rhinoceros, bison, bears, hyenas, reindeer, giant deer and lions.

Herds of bison roamed the tundra-like plain 50,000 years ago.

Ice Age hunters lived in caves from where they hunted and foraged for food.

Thor's Cave is one of many caves in the Manifold Valley where animal bones and artefacts have been found dating from the Ice Age.

Stone tools such as this worked flint point have been found across the Peak District.

At the height of the last Ice Age, about 18,000 years ago, the Peak District was just south of the towering glacial wall. The region's tundra landscape of iron hard ground and low growing vegetation was roamed across by herds of deer. Predators followed the deer, including people. Evidence for human life in the Peak District is tantalisingly rare and confined to the recesses of protective caves of the limestone White Peak. Ice Age finds have been made in at least ten caves, many in the Manifold Valley. These include stone tools used for hunting, butchery and other food preparation. Fragments of animal bones show that bear, reindeer and woolly mammoths lived amongst the Peak District hills. The most spectacular site is Creswell Crags, near Worksop, where a rich set of finds and environmental data has been discovered by archaeologists working in the many caves that penetrate the sides of a narrow gorge.

Stone tools found in and near caves testify to the presence of families during the last Ice Age.

Places to Visit

CRESWELL CRAGS

Creswell Crags is one of the most northerly inhabited places on earth during the last Ice Age. The Crags form a narrow gorge of steep limestone cliffs riddled with deep caves. Archaeologists began excavating here in the nineteenth century, finding stone tools and remains of animals who occupied the gorge during and immediately after the Ice Age. Excavations continued until the 1990s when the British Museum and University of Sheffield worked in Pin Hole Cave. Finds cover a massive time period, beginning some 130,000 years ago, long before the last Ice Age even began, until the Middle and New Stone Ages of 10,000 to 6000 years ago. The landscape changed dramatically during this time, going from near tropical conditions through the permafrost of the Ice Age to the more temperate climate we know today. Ice Age finds include stone arrowheads and butchery knives, the bones of woolly mammoths, woolly rhinoceros and giant deer, and a bone decorated with the carving of a horse. A discovery unique in Britain was made in 2003 when Britain's only known Ice Age rock art was found. All of the caves are now protected by metal grills to preserve the rare archaeological deposits inside.

This flint hand axe was made by a Neanderthal living at Cresswell between 250,000 and 25,000 years ago.

Above: *Cresswell Crags and the whole of the Peak District would have been a more tropical place 120,000 years ago.* Right: *The entrance to Robin Hood's Cave, the largest cave at Cresswell Crags.*

Start a visit at the Museum and Education Centre, situated at the east end of the gorge. The centre houses the excellent *Age of Ice* exhibition with cave tours and special events throughout the year. The Ice Age tour takes you to Robin Hood Cave, the largest at Creswell, while the rock art tour visits the newly discovered art in Church Hole Cave. There are also footpaths around the beautiful gorge. Visit the Creswell Heritage Trust website for further details including opening times – www.creswell-crags.org.uk

DIRECTIONS
Creswell Crags is between the towns of Mansfield and Worksop, on the border between Derbyshire and Nottinghamshire (SK534741).

The Manifold Valley is
framed by the spectacular
entrance to Thor's Cave.

THOR'S CAVE

The most prominent cave of the Manifold Valley is Thor's Cave, the entrance of which is in a dramatic limestone peak that rises high above the valley floor. The cave was formed when the valley floor was at the same level as the entrance over one million years ago and the river actually flowed out of the cave entrance. Erosion since then has created the valley and left the cave high above ground level. The cave formed as water flowed underground through small cracks so dissolving the limestone. The cave was once completely filled with water so creating the rounded arch at the top. The entrance is over 20 metres high and looks out over the valley like an omniscient eye. Ice Age stone tools, as well as Romano-British pottery and brooches, were found in the 1920s and 1930s by archaeologists excavating a number of the caverns in the cave system.

DIRECTIONS

Thor's Cave is visible from the Manifold Trail between Waterhouses and Hulme End (SK098549). You can reach the cave entrance along a steep footpath between the trail and nearby Wetton village.

ICE AGE

50,000 years ago –
10,000 years ago
48,000BC – 8000BC

Glaciers cover northern Europe

People live in small nomadic groups, travelling the permafrost south of the glaciers

First people arrive in Australia and New World

CHAPTER 2
Forest Nomads

Arctic-like tundra followed in the wake of the retreating glaciers over 10,000 years ago. The ground thawed and began to wake up. Then thick forests slowly colonised the land from the south, until within a few hundred years the Peak District was transformed from a bleak and forbidding place on the edge of the world to a landscape rich in life and possibilities.

Increasing numbers of nomadic families lived in the woodland. They moved with the seasons to visit places that offered opportunities to gather plants for food and hunt animals through spring to autumn and shelter over winter. The earliest communities journeyed between the Peak District hills and the surrounding lowlands, possibly as far away as the North Sea coast. Distances travelled became steadily shorter over the generations, until communities were more likely to move between the hills and the valleys within the Peak District and with more limited movement beyond the region. They have left scant traces in their wake, but one of the biggest legacies they have left was to start clearing the forests and so create the open moorlands we know today.

Movement of the People

The valleys were first dominated by pines after the ice, but later these were slowly replaced by deciduous species such as oak and elm. The forest probably covered all of the Peak District except for the highest ground in the High Peak and around Peak Forest. Though even these high altitudes, treeless today, would have been a scrub-land of birch, hazel and willow.

Flint tools such as these scrapers and blades were discarded or lost over 6000 years ago.

The first evidence for human life in the forest are finds of stone arrowheads, scrapers and knives. These were the tools needed to work and hunt. Two types of stone were used to make implements: flint and chert. Flint comes from outside the Peak District, the nearest sources being the Yorkshire Wolds and Cheshire Plain. Chert is found in limestone and is commonly seen eroding out of dalesides in the Wye Valley and Lathkill Dale. Obtaining these raw materials would have been an important part of the seasonal round. Tools were left behind where they were used or broken. An arrowhead that missed its target or a scraper broken when digging for plants. The most common finds are flakes of waste stone created while making tools that lie where they fell around a person sitting beside a camp fire.

The largest scatters of stone tools are found by river confluences or on edges overlooking valleys. These include at least three joinings of rivers in the Upper Derwent,

Flint tools and waste flakes have been found from nomadic hunting camps situated above edges and on low-lying ground above valleys such as these.

on moorland at Pike Lowe and Mickleden Edge, and at a riverside cave at Wetton Mill. All of these were places regularly visited by families over time, favoured for the resources they offered. Riversides supported a variety of edible seeds, tubers, greens, medicinal plants and herbs as well as attracting animals for water. People didn't restrict themselves to rivers. They moved between the higher ground and the valleys, at home in the forest and the lighter scrub, using the resources of both.

Fragile remains of a settlement have been found on Broomhead Moor. A ring of five stakeholes supported a windbreak near to a paved area and hearths surrounded by flints. It was radio-carbon dated to about 8500 years ago. Another settlement was discovered at Deepcar, just to the east of the Peak District. Quartzite blocks and sandstone flags were arranged in an oval pattern interpreted by the excavators as the possible footing of a windbreak. Within this was a roughly circular setting of gritstone blocks approximately 4 by 3m across, inside which were three hearths. A total of 23,000 flint and chert tools and waste flakes, most originating in the Yorkshire Wolds, were found inside and to the south of the shelters.

The moorlands we know today were created in prehistory as nomadic hunter-gatherers created woodland clearings to attract game.

The forest and scrub began to decline from approximately 7500 to 7000 years ago and blanket peat began to spread across the higher ground. This was the beginning of the peat moorlands. Some archaeologists interpret this as the result of climate change, wetter and colder weather encouraging the formation of peat. Others see people playing an important role in altering the environment. Finds of charcoal in peat deposits may be the remains of large fires set to create woodland clearings. Large game animals, such as deer, are attracted to the lusher vegetation of clearings, so making your own opening in the trees means you can attract animals to where you want them. Being able to predict where and when your food will appear makes hunting a lot easier. Whichever caused the decline in trees, the loss of upland habitats eventually made life more difficult and reduced the amount of food available in the uplands. Short-term gain led to a long-term loss. Perhaps there are lessons to be remembered.

Places to Visit

MIDDLE STONE AGE
(Mesolithic)
10,000 years ago –
6000 years ago
8000BC – 4000BC

Large Mammals become
extinct in Europe

Forests return to northern
Europe with warmer climate

People reach the southern
tip of South America

There are no sites to visit of this period, the faint traces of occupation leaving no enduring monuments. Collections of Middle Stone Age tools can be seen in the region's museums, including Sheffield and Buxton.

CHAPTER 3
First Farmers

The first people to raise livestock and tend crops built the earliest permanent monuments in Britain. Stone burial mounds, chambered tombs and henges were constructed across the landscape, the most famous being Stonehenge, Avebury and West Kennet Long Barrow in South West England. But many massive stone monuments were built across the British Isles and good examples are found in the Peak District. The desire to build at a monumental scale was strongly linked with the domestication of the wild that was an integral part of farming.

Fill the Hope Valley, seen here from Surprise View, with more trees and you can imagine how the Peak District valleys were forested over 4000 years ago.

Domesticating the World

Farming came to Britain nearly 6000 years ago. Changes in pottery and flint tools, as well as the building of monuments, were associated with this early agriculture, leading archaeologists to call the period of the first farmers the Neolithic, meaning New Stone Age. What was once seen as a sudden introduction of farming and new technology by settlers is now thought to have been the gradual adoption of new ways of living over hundreds of years. Communities came into contact with those who had adopted agriculture from others, possibly taking up certain new practices at different times rather than together as a single farming culture. Gathering, hunting and nomadic movement continued as central aspects of community life well into the New Stone Age. It was a slow domestication of the world. People living in the Middle Stone Age had to know when certain plants would fruit and seed, when deer would migrate and when animals would give birth. This knowledge was not abandoned with the adoption of agriculture, however the rearing of animals and crops required an even more precise knowledge of and involvement with seasonal life-cycles. Livestock had to successfully mate, seeds needed to be stored over winter and germinated in the spring if farming was to successfully provide food year after year.

Neolithic cattle were smaller and probably much hairier than modern breeds maybe being somewhat more reminiscent of Highland cattle.

The Origins of Farming

Farming originated in many parts of the world at different times. Breeding domestic livestock and cultivating plants was independently 'discovered' in the Middle East, Far East, Africa, the Pacific and the Americas. It was from early farming in the Middle East, which began about 11,000 years ago, that farming spread to Britain 5000 years later. Archaeologists debate whether agriculture was introduced by farming settlers from Europe or whether the knowledge, domestic breeds and crops were exchanged between communities – gatherer-hunters slowly adopting some elements of agriculture into their existing lifestyles. The latter is most likely.

People lived in small communities, largely made up of those related to each other by kin. They continued to live mobile lifestyles, with individual groups separated from each across a landscape still dominated by trees away from the moorlands. Movement was no longer only related to wild resources and the migrations of deer. People now began to move with their livestock between pastures and fields in different places as well as to the places good for hunting and gathering. Cattle and sheep would have grazed under trees in thinner patches of woodland or on pastures within clearings, some the result of repeated woodland management by fire. Crops would have been cultivated in similar locations. Forest and farming often mixed.

Polished and knapped flint axes such as these from Poole's Cavern appeared during the Neolithic after the introduction of farming.

It is rare to discover houses dating from this period in the Peak District, but two were excavated almost next to each other near Buxton in the 1980s. Archaeologists working in advance of building work found the post-holes of two rectangular timber buildings, free-standing posts, and pits containing charcoal and burnt stones from domestic fires. There were numerous flakes from the making of flint tools. One pit was radio-carbon dated to about 8000 years old, placing it in the Middle Stone Age, while the whole settlement was dated to the New Stone Age at approximately 5500 years ago. Environmental evidence preserved in peat, animal bones in pits and organic residues preserved on the inside of pot sherds showed that crops were cultivated, cattle reared for meat and dairy produce, wild apples harvested and honey taken from wild bee hives.

Neolithic burial mounds like this one at Pea Low near Alstonefield were built on prominent hills and ridges. These locations were deliberately chosen so that the dead ancestors could be visible from the surrounding landscape.

This stone-lined burial chamber would have been inside the massive mound on Minninglow.

Tombs of the Ancestors

These first farmers built massive stone burial mounds on the tops of hills and ridges across the limestone plateau. They are the commonest Neolithic monuments in the Peak District, with at least 19 sites surviving from between 5500 and 4500 years ago. Two different types of mound were built, long barrows and round barrows. Long barrows vary from between 30 and 50 metres long, some being oval mounds while others are up to three times longer than they are wide. Most round barrows are between 10 and 45 metres in diameter. Sites like Pea Low and Minninglow stand at over 3 metres high.

The nature of the tombs changed over time. The earliest monuments were circular mounds that contained one or more stone-lined chambers, such as at Five Wells, Green Low, Harboro Rocks and Minninglow. Low passages allowed access to the chambers of some tombs but not at others. These were later superseded by larger long barrows. Some sites had long and complex histories throughout the New Stone Age. Minninglow began life as a round chambered tomb which was enlarged and had more chambers added until it became a long barrow over 30 metres across. The unusually long monument at Long Low is a 200-metre stone bank that may have been added to a small chambered tomb.

Human skeletons, disjointed bones and cremations have been found underneath and inside all of the mounds. In some tombs, bones from numerous individuals were selected and placed inside stone-lined chambers. One tomb at Five Wells contained the bones of at least twelve people.

Most Neolithic burial chambers were capped with huge limestone slabs. The amount of effort required to quarry, move and position the slabs is just one indicator of the importance of the tombs.

Solomon's Tower is a gentleman's folly built on top of Grinlow, a Neolithic burial tomb above Poole's Cavern, Buxton.

The grave goods found in the burial mound on Liffs Low include two finely worked flint axes, a pair of boar's tusks, an antler macehead, haematite and a unique small clay pot dating from the Neolithic.

Why did Neolithic people undertake these vast construction projects, using such permanent and elaborate means to mark the burial places of their dead, when their forebears had not? In building the mounds at high altitudes, they were physically altering the earth. They raised the heights of hills, embellishing the natural landscape through physical labour. It was the further taming of the wild, turning natural places into enduring symbols of community identity. These high locations were probably upland pastures, cleared from amongst lighter woodland or scrubland. We think that communities moved between these pastures and the wooded valleys during the year, claiming access to land for settlement and farming by traditional right. The monuments and burials reinforced these rights.

Bodies were not interred as the result of simple funeral rites. Only certain people were chosen, perhaps important individuals or people who died at auspicious occasions. The dead are often accompanied by sets of fine objects including flint axes and pottery vessels. Some may have been made specially for the burials, others were possibly family heirlooms. Where we find the partial remains of different individuals mixed together, it is likely that the dead had been first exposed to the elements, carrion and predators. After the flesh had decayed or been eaten, certain bones were selected for burial inside the chambers. The dead had been turned into eternal ancestors.

Ancestral Ceremonies

As you stand next to one of these grass-covered tombs today, picture it as a mound of newly exposed bright, white limestone. It would have been visible across the surrounding landscape, from where the builders probably came. Anyone travelling or living within sight of the hill could not miss their ancestors looking down on them.

The ancestral tombs proclaimed the right to have access to the land from one community to another. The permanence of the mounds and the bones of ancestors would have reunited the community with the land each time they returned with their livestock. A number of chambers in a single mound may have housed ancestors of separate groups from within the same community. Or were these different communities who shared the same pasture and co-operated over the building of the mound?

Access into the tombs in Minninglow were originally kept open for ceremonies using the ancestral bones within. The mound was enlarged over time so that the tombs were eventually located deep inside the monument.

The prominent location chosen for the burial mound at Five Wells affords long-distance views to both north and south. With its original covering mound the tomb would have been a highly visible feature of the Neolithic landscape.

In the earlier part of the New Stone Age it was important that people could get into the tombs, to reach the decaying bodies and bare bones. Religious and community leaders could have crawled on hands and knees through the entrances and into the darkness. They would have conducted rites with the bones, possibly even bringing some bones outside to be used in ceremonies held in front of the gathered community. The impressive back-drop of the mound itself, heightened at Green Low by a façade of stone to either side of the entrance, and the way the surrounding landscape was laid out below, would have reinforced to participants their traditional connections with the land. Their place in the world and the ideal of common ancestry within the community was reaffirmed.

Good tombs to visit in the Peak District are Five Wells near Taddington, Pea Low near Alstonfield and the unusually lengthy mound on Long Low near Wetton. There is also an early tomb hidden below the later burial mound at Gib Hill near to Arbor Low.

Arbor Low henge and the adjacent Gib Hill long mound may have looked something like this early on, though Gib Hill may actually pre-date the henge.

Gatherings of People

Some of the most impressive of all prehistoric monuments are the large circular embanked enclosures known as henges, of which Stonehenge and Avebury in Wiltshire are the most famous in Britain. They were built between 6000 and 4000 years ago to hold large ceremonial gatherings.

Henges are distinctive in having a deep ditch within a large bank to enclose a circular, level area that is accessed by two opposing entrances. Many had long histories beginning as simple banks and ditches, with stone circles later built inside.

While the earlier tombs mimicked and embellished the natural topography, henges were designed along more formal and abstract architectural lines to create elaborate arenas for the holding of large ceremonies. The numbers of people congregating at the henges would have been much larger than those who had gathered at the earlier tombs.

Henges were enclosed within massive banks. These prevented anyone on the outside from seeing ceremonies held on the inside though it is likely that people stood on the banks to participate, separated from the ritual centre by the ditches.

Three of the large limestone slabs that once stood upright to form the stone circle inside the henge at Arbor Low. The stones now lie horizontally where they were pushed as if marking out the face of a clock.

There are two henges in the Peak District, Arbor Low near Youlgrave and the Bull Ring in Dove Holes. Both are approximately circular, 85 metres in diameter with 2 metre high banks. Only Arbor Low has a stone circle, the stones now laid flat on the ground. Today, they are dominated by their modern surroundings. Arbor Low is set amongst green fields of neatly cropped grass, divided by dry-stone walls. The Bull Ring is also covered in short grass, but here the similarity ends. Hemmed in by houses, a school and an abandoned quarry, the henge echoes to the sounds of traffic and children playing on the sports field.

Strip away these recent layers of time and you are walking across open landscapes that were a mix of lightly-grazed pasture and woodland. You're converging on a henge with your family, having helped to maintain the banks and clean the ditches of silt last year. Crowds of comparative strangers, possibly numbering hundreds of people gathered from across the region, are already milling outside the henge. Their camp fires ring the imposing earthen banks. The babble of voices rises and falls, mixing with the anxious calls of cattle and sheep. The repetitive chink of flint tools being made sings in the air. Mounting excitement grabs you, as again the chance to see distant cousins and participate in the large and complex ceremonies draws closer.

The formal ceremonies that drew the different communities would have been only one aspect of the gatherings. People also probably took part in feasts, exchanged cattle, flint nodules and polished stone axes, arranged marriage partners and debated access to land. There was the potential for conflicting claims to the same areas so gatherings could give the opportunity to negotiate and argue over where communities intended to go and what resources they would use. Most importantly, they renewed social bonds that connected them when apart for most of the year.

The high banks and the entrances controlled access to the rituals conducted inside the henges, heightening the ceremonial drama. We aren't sure whether everybody would have been allowed in or only important people such as shaman and community leaders. Some people may have only watched ceremonies from on top of the banks. When upright, the stone structure at the very centre of Arbor Low would have allowed just enough room for one or two people inside, while preventing others seeing what they were doing.

Both Peak District henges probably once contained stone circles that created elaborate spaces for conducting ceremonies. The circle at Arbor Low survives but has been pushed over.

ROCK ART

Prehistoric rock art is very difficult to date. The cups and rings pecked into gritstone boulders cannot be radio-carbon dated and are rarely found in association with dateable artefacts such as pottery. Archaeologists believe they date from the New Stone Age or Bronze Age. This is because boulders with rock art are often found re-used in later burial mounds. Good examples from the Peak District have been found in burial mounds at Barbrook and Eyam Moor and in the wall defending a 3000 year old settlement near Bakewell. Groups of small cup marks are common, often encircled with a carved ring. Gritstone is a soft rock susceptible to weathering and therefore the best examples of rock art are to be found in Weston Park Museum, Sheffield. One cup-marked boulder can be seen in a mound on Eyam Moor. A large flat boulder on Gardom's Edge shows a typical original rock art setting.

Places to Visit

PEA LOW

Pea Low is one of the best preserved and most impressive prehistoric chambered tombs in the Peak District. It is a massive stone cairn, approximately 40 metres in diameter and standing over 3 metres high. Located on the edge of a hilltop at 350m above sea level, there are beautiful views across Alstonefield, the Manifold Valley and Dovedale. Only to the north west does the land rise higher. The dramatic choice of location is obvious when you approach from the south west. Pea Low is visible on the skyline from the Alstonefield to Wetton road, just over 1 kilometre away. Look above the houses of Alstonefield and follow the limestone walls up to the horizon until you find the mound to the left of the trees. You really appreciate Pea Low's size from this distance. From Alstonefield itself the mound is hidden by the rising land until you have climbed up the slope and are close to it. Then it is abruptly revealed. This sudden appearance would have heightened the impact for those arriving here to participate in ancestor ceremonies.

Pea Low is one of the most impressive surviving Neolithic burial mounds in the Peak District.

Opposite page: *The cup-and-ring-marked boulder on Gardom's Edge is one of the more elaborate examples of prehistoric rock art in the Peak District.*

The excellent views from Pea Low take in the village of Alstonefield and the surrounding hills of the limestone plateau.

Thomas Bateman, Samuel Carrington and others excavated Pea Low in the 1840s, finding a human burial, a cremation, disjointed human bones and animal bones within the mound. The cairn continued to attract attention over time. Someone in the Roman period buried a hoard of over 50 coins. Later still, about 1400 years ago, a member of the local ruling classes was buried here, accompanied to the grave with an iron spear and a polished amber button.

Today, three dry-stone walls converge on its summit. These were built by 1839 and quarries dug into the side of the mound show what the wall builders thought the Neolithic tomb was useful for.

DIRECTIONS

Pea Low is 1km to the north of Alstonefield (SK131565). It can be reached by public footpaths from the village and makes a good destination for a short circular walk.

LONG LOW

A 200-metre-long stone and earth bank topped with a dry-stone field wall runs along almost the full length of a ridge above the Hamps Valley. At 30 metres wide and 3 metres high in places, Long Low is a very large and unusual prehistoric monument. It ends in mounds at the northern and southern ends, both of which are now higher than the rest of the bank because wall builders robbed stone from in between. Short, low stone banks extend out to either side from the front of the northern mound. These may be the remains of a façade that created a backdrop for ceremonies, though they are now difficult to see because of disturbance by lead miners, wall builders and Victorian antiquarians.

Look out from Long Low and you are struck by how high you feel in the world, the altitude could be at least another 1000 metres. You are surrounded by rising hills and ridges of farmland pasture dissected by limestone walls. Look closely at the hilltops

The aptly named Long Low is 200m long and runs along the top of a natural ridge.

Looking north east along the top of Long Low. Alstonefield and Pea Low are in the distance straight ahead.

and you will see the characteristic pimple like bumps of other burial mounds, most built about 1000 years after Long Low. Pea Low is visible to the north east.

Samuel Carrington excavated Long Low in 1848. He discovered that the earliest part of the monument was a dry-stone wall running the entire length of the bank. Stone slabs were leant against the wall before being covered with the stone and earth that forms the bulk of the bank. As Carrington dug into the northern mound he found a 2-metre-high stone chamber or passage grave containing over 13 complete burials, numerous disjointed human bones and large quantities of animal bones. More human and animal bones were buried in the body of the mound itself, accompanied by pottery, flint tools, leaf-shaped arrowheads and worked bone objects. Buried in the southern end of the bank were two or three rows of vertically set stone slabs, a human cremation and more animal bones.

DIRECTIONS

Long Low is approximately 2km to the south west of Alstonefield and a similar distance to the south east of Wetton (SK122539). You can get to within 100m of its southern end via a network of walled lanes and public footpaths from either village or from Ilam, 3km to the south. Two stiles in the field walls allow access on to the monument itself. This access is concessionary so please respect the farmland.

FIVE WELLS

To get an idea of what lay within the chambered cairns you should visit the twin tombs at Five Wells. As you walk uphill towards Five Wells, your first sight of the tomb is of grey limestone slabs above the adjacent field wall. The slabs stick out of the grass like worn teeth. They are placed on end to create two rectangular chambers that sit back-to-back and are aligned east to west. Each chamber is a rectangular stone box about 2 metres long and 1 metre wide, which would have originally been roofed with a thick limestone slab. Entrances face outwards, flanked either side by 1.5-metre-high upright posts. The eastern chamber survives in better condition with only the loss of its roof.

The chambers would have originally been buried from view, deep in the centre of a large earth and stone mound. Entrances on opposite sides of the mound provided access into the chambers from the outside. Most of this has been removed by wallers building the field wall that crosses to the north of the cairn and by Victorian antiquarians. The remains of the 20-metre-diameter mound still survive to 1 metre high. Each entrance led to a low, stone-lined passage that connected the world of the living with the chambers of the ancestors. Some time later in the New Stone Age or early in the Bronze Age, the cairn was buried in a larger mound that completely covered and blocked the entrances.

The tomb sits above a steep north-facing ridge that offers great views across the limestone plateau. You can see down into the Wye Valley and as far north as Bradwell Moor. Springs issue from just below the ridge, hence the name 'Five Wells'.

The entrances to the chambers at Five Wells are 'guarded' by two upright posts. There would have originally been a slab covering the whole tomb.

The two back-to-back burial chambers at Five Wells are exposed because most of the stone covering the mound has since been removed. The well-preserved east facing chamber is in the foreground with the other chamber just visible behind.

Thomas Bateman was the first antiquarian to excavate Five Wells, digging part of the cairn in 1846. Others followed throughout the reign of Queen Victoria. One chamber was full of the bones of at least twelve men and women. Inside the other chamber there were three complete skeletons accompanied with sherds of Neolithic pottery vessels.

DIRECTIONS
Five Wells is 2km west of Taddington (SK124710). There is a concessionary path to the tomb from Pillwell Lane, which runs north from the Taddington to Chelmorton road approximately 300 metres to the west of Five Wells. This path can be reached along public footpaths from either Taddington or Chelmorton, though there is nearer parking on Pillwell Lane. Follow the home-made wooden signs from the road.

ARBOW LOW AND GIB HILL

Arbor Low henge comes into view ahead of you when you cross the second wall beyond the farmhouse. I recommend that you don't head straight for the imposing earthen bank, but go to the left and find one of the original entrances. Enter the henge in the footsteps of those who built it to get an impression of how it would have appeared to the Neolithic communities gathered here for ceremonies.

Inside Arbor Low there is ring of 50 limestone blocks and, at the very centre, seven more stones forming a cove. All of the stones are now fallen, possibly pushed over by superstitious farmers. They originally stood to between 1.6 and nearly 3 metres tall, with the larger stones by the entrances and at the cove. The stone circle was probably added later to the existing henge, and may have replaced a wooden circle.

If entering the henge 4000 years ago you would have been confronted by these impressive standing stones creating a picket fence between you and activities happening inside. You would then have to pass between two of the stones to enter the inner ceremonial space. The grey limestone ring would form one of two

This is how Arbor Low and nearby Gib Hill burial mound may have looked like during a ceremony later in the history of the two monuments.

Arbor Low henge from the top of the later burial mound built on top of the henge bank.

barriers to the outside world, the other being the outer bank. With the world cut off from view your attention would be focused on the towering structure in the middle, standing at least half again in height as yourself. Picture the equivalent of priests or elders leading ceremonies, the banks lined with people. Would they be silent or chanting? Smells of wood smoke, possibly cooking meat, drift through the air. You might be expectantly waiting for midsummer or midwinter sunrise, sunset or moonrise. The sky could be a clear carpet of stars or lost under thick cloud. You're waiting for the signs, the omens, the predicted natural event that renews the year. You might be nervous or confident that they will appear; they are fundamentally important to the well-being of the society you live in, their timing fully understood. Arbor Low was a very different place to that of today.

A large burial mound was built on the bank next to the northern entrance. It dates from when the henge with its stone circle was still in use or possibly shortly after. This was no accidental over-development of part of the henge. The people responsible for deliberately placing the mound right on the bank were clearly augmenting the existing bank whilst maintaining the sanctity of the internal ceremonial space.

The burial mound built later on Arbor Low henge stands out against the skyline to the left.

They were claiming an ancestral line from one of the largest ceremonial sites in the Peak District. We can't be sure whether this was one kin group's attempt at dominance over the others or a more communal decision to incorporate changing funerary practices into ceremonies at Arbor Low. What is important is that the burial mound builders very clearly brought the display of their own ancestors right into the henge, perhaps to link themselves with the original henge builders.

The two opposing entrances have very different views. Whilst the one facing south east looks onto rising ground, the north-west entrance faces out across the limestone plateau. There are good views from the second entrance across a shallow valley and the village of Monyash. This view was the wider backdrop to those gathering around the henge 4000 years ago.

Arbor Low was excavated in 1901 and 1902 by H. St George Gray who placed trenches next to the cove, across the ditches and through the banks to either side of the southern entrance. He discovered a human burial next to the cove, as well as ox teeth, red deer antler, a flint scraper and an arrowhead in the ditches. Thomas

Bateman excavated the mound built on the bank in 1845 and nearby Gib Hill in 1848 when he found the stone burial chamber containing a small Food Vessel, flint tools and burnt human bones. The vessel and watercolours are now in Weston Park Museum, Sheffield. Fieldwalking in the vicinity of the henge has produced many New Stone Age and early Bronze Age stone tools and waste flakes including polished stone axes from Cumbria and a round hammerstone. These were probably left behind by the people gathering at Arbor Low, some the remains of camps.

Gib Hill long barrow may be dominated today by Arbor Low henge, but it shouldn't be overlooked. Gib Hill, which supposedly takes its name from its use for a gibbet, was the earliest focus for ceremonies, pre-dating Arbor Low by at least several centuries. The builders scattered oxen bones and buried cremated human bones in layers within the mound. In the right light, you can make out shallow hollows scooped out of the ground around Gib Hill. These were dug to quarry the bedrock used to build the mound.

THE VICTORIAN AND THE PLUMMETING TOMB

When the antiquarian Thomas Bateman excavated Gib Hill in 1848, he didn't realise that there were two mounds of different periods superimposed on each other. He decided to tunnel into the mound from the side, hoping to gain access to the burials he expected to find at ground level. Nearing the centre of the cairn, his workmen were surprised to notice a large stone slab in the roof of his tunnel. This was the floor of the Bronze Age stone-lined tomb which collapsed into the tunnel. Bateman's workmen escaped just in time. Bateman moved the tomb to his garden and it was only reconstructed and replaced inside Gib Hill in 1938.

Gib Hill rises above the skyline. It is actually two prehistoric mounds built one-on-top of the other.

What you see today is actually two mounds built one-on-top of the other. The height of Gib Hill was increased several centuries later in the Bronze Age when a round burial mound was built on top of the earlier grave. If you look carefully, the gentler profile of the earlier cairn can be seen extending to the north east of the more prominent Bronze Age mound. Climb on top of Gib Hill and you will see the top stone slab of the second mound's burial chamber. Bateman found a Food Vessel and a cremation inside the chamber.

DIRECTIONS

The henge is 350m from a car park just off the B5055, 5km west of Youlgrave (SK160636). Gib Hill is about 260m south west of Arbor Low. There are interpretation panels at the approaches to the henge and Gib Hill. Access is through a farmyard, for which there is a small charge. An illustrated booklet about Arbor Low and Gib Hill is available for sale at the farm and Bakewell Visitor Centre.

BULL RING

The Bull Ring is almost the same size as Arbor Low, though without the stone circle. The bank survives as a major earthwork though it was originally twice its current height. The ditch has been partly filled but can still be traced on the ground. One stone was described standing inside the henge in 1789, thought then to be the only survivor of a complete ring. Excavations in 1949 did not find any evidence for foundation holes to support the stones, so it is still unknown whether there ever was a complete circle or not.

Hills rise on all sides around the henge which is built where a narrow valley widens out to form an area of level ground. The monument's two opposed entrances are oriented north to south and aligned on the valley.

The Bull Ring would have been as important a place for communal gatherings as was Arbor Low though it was not built with such long-distance views in mind. The

The Bull Ring Neolithic henge from outside the south-facing entrance.

hills restrict the view to the immediate valley. The size of the henge and its similarity to Arbor Low indicate that it would have been as important a place for large communal gatherings from the surrounding region. It is as if the builders deliberately chose the valley to find a natural landscape that mimicked the shape of a henge. This is further suggested by the alignment of the entrances along the valley. Perhaps the valley was an important communication route well travelled by nomadic farmers.

There is a burial mound about 25m south west of the henge, near to the southern entrance. As at Arbor Low, this would have been built as a funerary monument sometime after the henge was first created but when still used for ceremonies.

DIRECTIONS
The henge is within the village of Dove Holes, approximately 200m from the A6 (SK078783). Walk along the drive towards the sports clubhouse field and turn right. The henge is found next to the clubhouse.

NEW STONE AGE
(Neolithic)
6000 years ago –
4000 years ago
4000 BC – 2000 BC

Farming developed in
Middle East and Peru

Metalworking begins in Turkey

Stonehenge and Avebury built

Writing, the wheel and cities
invented in Middle East

CHAPTER 4
Dead Ringers

There is a massive increase in prehistoric monuments towards the end of the New Stone Age. The numbers of burial mounds increase so dramatically, from a few large tombs to hundreds of much smaller mounds, it is almost as if every one started burying their dead under a mound. Excavation has also found burials in flat graves unmarked by mounds. Many stone circles were built over the same time period. These funerary monuments and circles were built during a period of about 1000 years, between 4500 to 3500 years ago. This shows that there was a change in the scale of ceremonies and burial practices, with perhaps families or smaller related groups of families taking greater control than previously and building their own monuments. Large communal gatherings still continued at the henges and Arbor Low's own stone circle may have been added at this time, as were the first stones at Stonehenge.

This shift occurs at about the same time as metalworking is introduced into Britain. The first worked metals were gold and copper approximately 4000 to 4700 years ago. Metalworking skills were brought into Britain from continental Europe, where copper had already been worked for almost 2000 years. Metals did not replace flint and stone tools. Flint continued as a major raw material for making tools for at least another 1000 years. There are even some flint daggers and axes that are copies of new styles made in copper. Bronze working was discovered when tin was added to copper to make harder implements, and it arrived in Britain about 4000 years ago. Most of these early metal objects were axes, daggers and awls but strangely many were never used or sharpened. Jewellery such as bracelets, beads, rings and pendants were also made from gold and bronze. Many implements and weapons were buried with the dead or thrown into rivers and bogs as offerings to gods. It is as if the practical advantages of metal were not as important as other reasons for moulding bronze implements. Obtaining, exchanging and keeping these rare and precious objects were what was

Standing stones and stone circles were erected throughout Britain during the later part of the Neolithic and the early Bronze Age about 4500 to 3500 years ago.

important. They were as much designed for display as symbols of prestige and power than as functional weapons and tools. Bronze did come to replace polished stone as the material of choice for axes during the Bronze Age.

The raw materials of bronze, tin and copper ores, were mined in various places in the British Isles. South West England was an important source of both tin and copper, while copper alone was mined in southern Ireland, Wales, Cheshire and at Ecton in the Peak District. Miners used fires and antler picks to mine the ore from seams up to 70 metres below the ground. Hammerstones and an antler pick radio-carbon dated to about 3500 years ago found deep inside Ecton prove that there was early Bronze Age copper mining. The mine followed ore seams that delved under-ground into the limestone beside the Manifold Valley.

Bronze working appears alongside a new style of pottery known as Beaker ware that is commonly found in burial mounds across the whole of Europe. Beakers are usually tall, with an open mouth and decorated with intricate designs of pressed and incised lines. It was once thought that the 'Beaker' people were a distinct ethnic population who colonised Europe. In reality, objects, people, skills and knowledge had been moving large distances across Europe for generations and there were probably never individual waves of mass migrations just the constant movement of smaller groups of people and ideas. The discovery of a richly furnished burial near Stonehenge shows that certain individuals could and did move great distances to settle in new areas. The 'archer' was a male who was buried along with archery equipment and metalworking tools about 4300 years ago. Analysis of his teeth indicates that he spent a large part of his childhood somewhere in the Alps rather than southern Britain.

Pots were placed with burials towards the end of the Neolithic. These small pottery vessels sometimes contained cremations such as this one which was placed upside down and rested on top of a stone in a pit near Beeley, Derbyshire.

Circles of Life and Death

Henges had already been in existence for up to 2000 years when much smaller stone circles were built across the Peak District. At least 26 stone circles survive in the region today compared to only two henges. They either comprise small circles of standing stones that are usually set into a low bank or continuous banks of earth

Opposite: *Stone circles were built by families as special places to hold cere-monies that may have been tied to the seasons or phases of the moon.*

There are many accessible stone circles in the Peak District such as Nine Ladies on Stanton Moor.

One stone is usually larger than the others in Peak District stone circles. They are placed on the side of the circle that has a long-distance view. This stone is on the south-western side of the circle known as the Seven Stones of Hordron and is clearly positioned to form a line of sight with nearby Winhill for anyone standing inside or on the other side of the circle.

and stone known as ring cairns. Some ring cairns have been built around standing stones. The circles and ring cairns are between 9 and 30 metres across. The stones tend to be relatively short. Most are less than 1 metre high, with the exception of the 2-metre-high stones of Nine Stone Close. Nine Ladies on Stanton Moor is perhaps the best known and visited circle in the Peak District but other great examples are Seven Stones of Hordron, Wet Withens on Eyam Moor, Froggatt Edge and a group near Barbrook on the Eastern Moors.

One stone in the circle is often higher than the others. When you visit stone circles you should look out for where in the surrounding landscape can be seen from them. Many are built where rising land restricts good views to only one direction. The tallest stone is almost always on the side of the circle that faces this view.

The smaller size of stone circles and increase in numbers indicates the development of new ceremonies in addition to the large communal gatherings held at henges. Stone circles added another dimension to ceremonies rather than the immediate replacement of one with the other.

Stone circles are found near to settlements and fields so were probably built by individual families or small communities of related kin. They would have held their own ceremonies at the circles, possibly to mark the changing seasons and the farming year. Midwinter, spring, midsummer and harvest would have been important times for people who were closely connected to the land. Births, marriages and deaths may also have been celebrated. Some circles contain burials, the only one of these events to leave identifiable archaeological traces.

Living with your Ancestors

At the same time as stone circles were becoming the foci for family ceremonies, communities started to bury individuals in round mounds. These mounds were much smaller and built in different sorts of places than the earlier chambered tombs and long barrows of the New Stone Age. While the earlier tombs were placed on highly prominent hill tops and ridges with long-distance views over large tracts of landscape, the later mounds are just as likely to be found in locally prominent locations. Like the stone circles, they were probably built by families or small communities who lived nearby.

On the surface the mounds look fairly simple, but this hides a great diversity of buried structures and deposits. There are often internal stone kerbs, stone boxes known as cists and deep graves. Many mounds were enlarged several times, with

A large stone burial mound near to the Barbrook 1 stone circle on Big Moor. There is an extensive landscape of circles, mounds and field boundaries dating from between 4500 to almost 2000 years ago on this moorland.

burials being added during different phases of activity. Funerary rites vary too. Sometimes the dead are buried, while at other times they are cremated first and their ashes placed in cists, pits or large pots known as beakers. Funerary goods are often placed with them. Common objects are simple pots, stone or bone tools and ornaments, while more fancy goods include rare finds of jewellery and bronze daggers. Though mounds often contain more than one person, burial emphasises the individual rather than the mixing of bones from different people.

Even though there are over 500 burial mounds in the Peak District, there are not enough burials for the 1000 or so years that the mounds were built. It is clear that certain people were being specially chosen for burial in these highly visible mounds. Were they local rulers or other individuals chosen to become ancestors? The simple grave goods found with most burials don't suggest high status people, so it is more likely that representatives of the community were chosen for special burial. The prominent mounds would constantly remind the living of their dead. In a time before title deeds and property ownership, this would reinforce a community's

Many burial mounds are found on locally prominent hilltops such as Wigber Low near Carsington. This complicated site began as a platform for exposing the dead to the elements at least 4000 years ago and was used again in the Anglian period for burials.

Burial mounds in the Peak District were built of stone and were often contained with substantial kerbs of carefully placed larger stones.

62

connections to the area they lived in and farmed. You could justify your right to occupy the land because you had buried your ancestors here.

Beakers have been found in a number of Peak District burial mounds. Two other styles of pottery were also placed with burials 400 years after Beakers were first introduced. These are known as Collared Urns and Food Vessels and were in use until about 3400 years ago. Collared Urns and Food Vessels are rarely found in the same burial mound, and on the rare occasions they are the Urns were buried after the Vessels. In the Peak District, Beakers are found in burials on the White Peak, Collared Urns on the Dark Peak and Food Vessels in both areas. We still don't know why the earlier Beakers are restricted to the limestone, except that they indicate that the earliest changes in funerary practices occurred on the White Peak where the earlier chambered tombs were built.

The shift in scale from the larger tombs to the smaller mounds, their proliferation in numbers and the choice of less-prominent locations for some of the mounds may be associated with a gradual settling down. Communities may have slowly become less nomadic when compared with the first farmers. Families who had travelled to the limestone for burials and ceremonies may have found their own local places to bury their dead and hold ceremonies by the time Collared Urns, Food Vessels and stone circles were in use. This does not mean that they became completely sedentary but that they travelled over shorter distances.

There are many burial mounds worth visiting in the Peak District including Wigber Low which was used for funerals in the New Stone Age, Bronze Age and Anglo-Saxon period. Pike Low in the Upper Derwent, the burial platform below the Three Men cairns on Gardom's Edge, a burial mound built right on top of Arbor Low, Gib Hill and numerous examples near Barbrook and on Stanton are all worth exploring. Unusual burial monuments are the square mound of Hob Hurst's House and the triple cairn on Beeley Moor.

Simple clay pots often accompany burials, such as this one which contained a cremated body and was buried in a pit on the Eastern Moors. The sequence of events that formed the funeral went from death and preparation of the body to cremation, placement of the ashes in the pot and then the burial of the pot in the ground. By doing this the family transported the individual from the world of the living to the world of the dead.

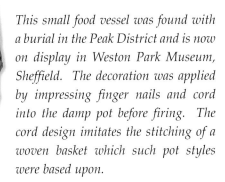

This small food vessel was found with a burial in the Peak District and is now on display in Weston Park Museum, Sheffield. The decoration was applied by impressing finger nails and cord into the damp pot before firing. The cord design imitates the stitching of a woven basket which such pot styles were based upon.

WHERE WAS EVERYONE ELSE BURIED?

The majority of people weren't given such enduring tombs when they died. They may have been buried in less permanently marked graves or left exposed to the elements. In 1995, archaeologists digging above Gardom's Edge found a cremation that had been buried about 2200 BC. It was placed in a small pit with a small wooden structure erected above the grave. The burial would probably have never been found except that the archaeologists were digging a much later round house that had fortuitously been built above it. At Wigber Low and Longstone Edge platforms were built on the tops of hills specifically to expose dead bodies. Corpses decayed in the open, attacked by carrion and carnivores. Though this may seem undignified to modern eyes, it is one way to allow the soul to leave the physical body, to let the deceased leave the world of the living for that of the dead.

RADIO-CARBON DATES

Many of the dates given in this book are based on radio-carbon dates. Radio-carbon analysis is an important dating method for archaeologists. All living things contain carbon. There's quite a bit in your body which is continually renewed by what you eat. Plants take up carbon dioxide during photosynthesis which is then passed to herbivores and from herbivores to carnivores. When people, animals or plants die no more carbon is added to the body, in fact it begins a long, slow process of decline. The rate of this decline is known which gives archaeologists the ability to measure the amount of carbon remaining in a piece of preserved plant or animal tissue. We can then get an approximate date for when the plant or animal died. Charcoal, bone, seeds and even pieces of preserved cloth or hair can be radio-carbon dated. Preservation is best when the object has been buried under peat or burnt. Dating isn't specific enough to give the exact year this happened, but gives a range of years that might be as many as a hundred or more. Even this accuracy is pretty good when we're talking about something – or somebody – over 2000 years old.

Places to Visit

STANTON MOOR

Stanton Moor contains a vast prehistoric landscape. The most spectacular is Nine Ladies stone circle; however, burial mounds, timber round houses, fields and clearance cairns survive below the heather and grass. There are a total of four stone circles and ring cairns on the moor. Many of these features can be seen from the footpath that runs between the Cork Stone in the south of the moor to the Tower. Look either side of the path for lumps and bumps amongst the heather. These are burial mounds, clearance cairns and ring cairns. Explore these lumps and discover the remains of the dead and living that are at least 3,000 years old.

The King Stone is an outlying stone of Nine Ladies. It is carved with the name Bill Stump, a reference to Pickwick Papers *by Charles Dickens.*

Despite its name, ten stones originally stood at Nine Ladies. One of the stones had fallen in the past and become hidden under the turf until its location was identified during the 1976 drought. The stones are set in a low bank to create a circle over 11 metres in diameter. The bank is now much lower than originally due to erosion but it

The beautiful setting for Nine Ladies stone circle is amongst birch woodland on Stanton Moor. This popular circle is easily reached by footpath and forms just part of a prehistoric landscape of ceremonial monuments, burial mounds, fields and round house sites.

can still be made out connecting the stones. According to Thomas Bateman there was a small burial mound built into the circle's bank which was excavated in 1787 to discover four clay urns containing cremations. There is another standing stone, known as the King Stone, 40 metres to the south west of the circle. This has the name Bill Stump above a cross and a circle engraved on it. Mr Pickwick in Charles Dickens's *Pickwick Papers* finds a stone engraved with 'Bill Stumps His Mark' which Pickwick describes as 'This treasure must be at once deposited where it can be thoroughly investigated, and properly understood.' He enthusiastically presents his findings to the Royal Antiquarian Society. Did Dickens visit Stanton Moor and be inspired by the graffiti or was the carving gouged into the King's Stone by a later reader of the *Pickwick Papers*? Dickens did visit the Peak District on at least one occasion…

Due to ongoing erosion, English Heritage funded a rescue and research excavation of Nine Ladies in 2003 but found little evidence apart from the standing stones. Antiquarians and amateur archaeologists excavated many of the burial mounds on Stanton in the eighteenth, nineteenth and early twentieth centuries. Many contained human cremations inside Beakers, Collared Urns or Food Vessels.

Three of Stanton Moor's Nine Ladies.

So who were the Nine Ladies? Like the names of many stone circles, Nine Ladies comes from folklore. The nine standing stones are reputedly nine women caught dancing on a Sunday and turned to stone in punishment. Their fiddler became the King Stone. We don't know when the name was first used, but the Church excommunicated anyone caught dancing during Sunday services from at least the 1500s. The medieval Church linked stone circles with devil worship in its attempt to end paganism. The name does prove that the tenth stone had fallen before the legend was created, possibly even in prehistory.

DIRECTIONS

Stanton Moor is approximately 4km to the south east of Bakewell near the villages of Stanton-in-Peak and Birchover (SK249635). There is limited road-side parking on Lees Road, though the moor makes for a good half day walk from Birchover. The moor is open access though the most notable sites can be seen from signposted footpaths. There are a number of interpretation panels that have reconstruction drawings of ceremonies at Nine Ladies.

ROBIN HOOD'S STRIDE AND NINE STONE CLOSE

Robin Hood's Stride is an outcrop of gritstone crowned with two natural towers. The distinctive rock formation has attracted activity and myths for a long time. A carved cup and ring mark on a horizontal surface might be prehistoric rock art, while timber round houses huddled around the rock during the Roman period. It was linked with Robin Hood and the Green Man in medieval times. It is also known as the Mock Beggars Hall because of the towers' likeness to chimney stacks.

Three hundred metres to the north of Robin Hood's Stride is a stone circle called Nine Stone Close. The four surviving stones, out of an original eight or nine, are the tallest of any stone circles in the Peak District at over 2 metres high. One of the stones is distinctively wider at the top than the bottom. Seven stones still stood in the Victorian period, the rest probably being taken away for use in buildings.

One of the impressive gritstone standing stones of Nine Stone Close.

Nine Stone Close stone circle. Four of the original stones survive in place, a fifth is in a field wall nearby. Robin Hood's Stride is in the distance.

There is a large stone built into the field wall to the south of the circle that was almost certainly one of the original stones. It was either moved from the circle or was another outlying 'Kings Stone' as at Nine Ladies. Thomas Bateman describes two standing stones about 80 metres south of the circle of which this could be one. The name comes from the surrounding field. Fields enclosed with walls were often called closes to differentiate them from open fields. This suggests that nine stones remained upright whenever the field was enclosed, possibly 300 to 400 years ago.

The circle is one of only a few in the Peak District that is not built into an earth or stone bank. The stones are erected in shallow pits in the ground. There is a slight mound within the stones which may be a platform or burial mound.

The proximity of the stone circle to Robin Hood's Stride is probably deliberate. The midsummer moon rises between the two towers when seen from Nine Stone Close. There are also good views to the north from the circle which is built on a slight ridge.

DIRECTIONS
Nine Stone Close is 2km south west of Stanton Moor (SK225626). There is no right of way to the stone circle itself but you can gain access from a nearby foot-path between Harthill Moor and Robin Hood's Stride. If you visit the circle please respect the surrounding farmland.

SEVEN STONES OF HORDRON

The Seven Stones of Hordron contains 10 standing stones forming a circle 15 metres across. It is one of the few free-standing circles with no bank in the Peak District. Located on high moorland 340 metres above sea level behind Hordron Edge, there are stunning views to the west. The distinctive shape of Winhill breaks the skyline 3.5km away. Some people have suggested that one of the stones was chosen because it is the same shape as Winhill's outline. The similarity is unconvincing, but Winhill and the high moorland would have formed a spectacular backdrop to ceremonies held here. The circle used to lie on the boundary between Yorkshire and Derbyshire, and was used as a landmark as early as Elizabethan times. In 1574 the county border ran 'to a place where certaine stones are sett upon the ends and having marks upon them called the Seavenstones'.

The slight remains of clearance cairns and field boundaries survive on the moors to the north and south of the circle. Seven Stones of Hordron may have been used by the community who lived and farmed this high land.

Seven Stones of Hordron overlooks the Derwent Valley with good views to Winhill and the High Peak moors in the distance. There are the remains of prehistoric fields and settlements nearby.

DIRECTIONS

The circle (SK 215868) is a 600m walk over rough moorland from Cutthroat Bridge car park on the A57. Follow the rough track until you reach the margin of the plantation then turn left and walk up the steep slope of Hordron Edge. The circle is about 50 metres behind the Edge.

FROGGATT EDGE STONE CIRCLE

This is an embanked stone circle or ring cairn built close to the top of Froggatt Edge. A bank of earth and stone was built around a ring of standing stones to form a 15-metre-diameter circle. Entrances were placed on opposite sides of the circle, at the south west and north east. The north-east entrance has been deliberately blocked with dry-stone walling, possibly a prehistoric modification of the circle.

Twelve stones survive today, though originally there would have been more. Most are about 0.5 metres tall, except for one of the stones framing the south-west entrance which is over 1 metre. This is the most impressive part of the circle surviving today. Four stones are set on the inner edge of the bank, showing that the stones were probably erected first and the bank built around them.

The circle is on the northern edge of a prehistoric landscape of small fields defined by low stone banks and clearance cairns. The surviving fields run for approximately one kilometre south of the circle. There are also several barrows in the vicinity.

The largest stone of Froggatt Edge stone circle marks one side of the entrance that faces the Derwent Valley. The rest of the circle is a continuous low wall.

There are very good views south west across the Derwent Valley towards the limestone plateau and the approximate location of sunset.

DIRECTIONS

The circle (SK 249768) is about 20 metres to the east of the footpath along the top of Froggatt Edge, just on the southern edge of a birch woodland. The largest stone is visible from the footpath.

WIGBER LOW

A stone cairn much like any other prehistoric burial mound covers the distinctive limestone knoll of Wigber Low. When the University of Sheffield excavated the site in the 1970s and 1980s they found evidence for a long and complicated history.

The story begins with the hill visited regularly in the New Stone Age. Flint tools and flakes created during tool manufacture suggest a temporary settlement occupied by a family of farmers who moved around the landscape with the seasons. Finds of stone hand axes made from stone quarried in Cumbria, North Wales and Leicestershire show that they participated in long-distance exchange networks.

Then later generations decided to build a large stone platform on top of the hill approximately 4000 years ago. Small human bones, such as knuckles, and the bones of carrion were found by archaeologists in the gaps between the stones. The remains of over 21 individuals survived. This platform had been used to lay out the dead, exposing their rotting corpses to the elements and carrion. Rats and crows would have feasted on the bodies, pulling away flesh and dragging some of the small bones away from the corpses. A stench of death would have hung above Wigber Low. This may seem a gruesome experience to us used to modern funeral services but such exposure is found in a number of cultures across the world. Buddhists in the Himalayas famously expose their dead on wheel shaped platforms known as sky burials. It is a way to release the spirit or soul of the dead person, to enable the individual to pass from the world of the living to that of the dead. Once defleshed, bodies would have been taken down to the surrounding area for burial. This is why archaeologists found only small bones and no larger leg or arm bones and no skulls. The smaller bones had fallen or been dragged down into the platform while the larger bones had been collected for burial.

Within a thousand years the stone burial mound you see today was built over the exposure platform. At least three skeletons and a cremation were discovered in this cairn, along with polished shale rings and beads. The knoll had itself become a place for burials.

The Low was used again for funerary rites over 2000 years later, when the bodies of local rulers were buried with spears, knives and brooches in the seventh century AD. At least five burials were inserted into the Bronze Age cairn. One was a double burial of a man between forty-five and fifty years and a woman between twenty-five and thirty years old. This burial was rich with grave goods. A sword was placed between the man and woman. Each had a small iron knife, while the woman was accompanied by a spearhead placed above her head and several decorated

This stone funerary platform is on top of Wigber Low near Bradbourne village in the south east of the Peak District.

A stone platform and burial mound survives on top of Wigber Low limestone knoll. It was used for funerary rites between 4,000 and 1,300 years ago.

bronze strips near her waist. These strips originally held together a small wooden purse that would have been attached to her belt. Lying across her left thigh were seven cow ribs; the remains of a joint of beef. Spearheads are common Anglo-Saxon funerary objects, usually buried with men. Another pit was dug into the southern edge of the cairn for the burial of a young woman aged between seventeen and twenty-five years. She was buried with a small orb of rock crystal. Orbs were popular amulets or good luck charms during the Anglo-Saxon period. Other interesting seventh-century finds were two almost identical beaver tooth pendants. Both were set in decorated short gold tubes. The most poignant burial was of a woman and a young child.

The Low is highly visible from the surrounding area and offers amazing views across the rolling limestone landscape. The distinctive outline of the trees planted on Minninglow chambered tomb break the north-east horizon.

DIRECTIONS

Wigber Low is 5km north east of Ashbourne (SK204514). You can reach the knoll via a public footpath between Kniveton village and the B5056 or from Bradbourne.

BARBROOK

The heather moorland on Big Moor, either side of Barbrook's coursing stream, is full of cairns and boundaries surviving from prehistoric farming. Some of the larger cairns are burial mounds placed close to the fields. Amongst them is one of the largest groups of stone circles and ring cairns in the Peak District. There are five, all within a few hundred metres of each other. The best preserved are known as Barbrook 1 and Barbrook 2.

Barbrook 1 stone circle is built on a platform that has been terraced into the sloping moorland. Families living nearby built the circle for small ceremonies.

Barbrook 1 is a wide circle of 12 standing stones set along the inner edge of an almost continuous stone and earth bank. The stones are all under 1 metre high except for one on the south-western side which faces a beautiful view across the Derwent Valley and the limestone plateau. This direction was deliberately emphasised by the builders of the circle by choosing this location. The land on the other sides gently rises to form a natural arena.

Barbrook 2 stone circle is about 300 metres north of Barbrook 1. Both are hidden from each other by the rolling moorland. Similar in size and with good views to the south west, ten stones are built into a circular dry-stone wall about 0.5m high. You can see how the sloping ground has been terraced inside the circle to create a level platform for ceremonies. Again, a stone on the south-western side is taller than the others. The circle is entered through a wide gap in the north east, which had been blocked with a low stone cairn some time in prehistory. The circle surrounds a small stone cairn in the centre. This circle shows the importance of the landscape to those holding ceremonies, those entering the circle seeing the view across the limestone plateau.

The circle was excavated in the 1960s. Four stones decorated with prehistoric cup marks and a burial pit under the central cairn were found. The pit contained a cremation buried in a large Collared Urn with a flint knife and scraper about 3500 years ago. The finds are now at Weston Park Museum, Sheffield. The circle was restored by the Peak District National Park Authority after being damaged in the 1980s.

The moorland around the circles is dotted with stone cairns. You can find many of these by walking between the two stone circles and by exploring the slope overlooking Barbrook. Some of these may have contained burials though no funerary evidence was found during excavations of three cairns in the 1960s. Flat gritstone slabs were placed around the mounds showing purposeful construction rather than just the dumping of stone cleared from fields for cultivation. A polished stone axe from Cumbria was found during the excavations. The stone cairns and mounds are part of a much larger prehistoric landscape that includes fields, houses and cairns on the west side of Barbrook – see Chapter 6.

The small cairn inside Barbrook 2 stone circle may have held burials.

DIRECTIONS

Barbrook 1 and 2 are on open access moorland 300 metres west of the A621. Follow the track from a layby next to a white gate. Barbrook 1 (SK279756) is just to the east of the track. From here follow a narrow path up slope to the large cairn then turn left to continue along the path north to Barbrook 2 (SK278758). You will pass two small cairns with kerbs. If you cross the moorland from Barbrook 2 back towards the track you will spot a number of grass covered mounds above the heather. These are burial mounds or large clearance cairns that still have holes in them from Antiquarian excavations. The track is a short walk from these mounds. Three other stone circles are north east of Barbrook Reservoir (SK283773), to the west of Barbrook (SK270752) and on the eastern side of the A621 (SK294748).

Barbrook 2 stone circle is a continuous low gritstone wall with a north-east facing entrance. It was deliberately built to give people entering the circle a long-distance view down the Derwent Valley.

Hob Hurst's House is a unique 4000-year-old burial mound. It is square and has this stone-lined square pit in its top.

One of the gritstone boulders erected to mark the line of Wet Withens stone circle.

HOB HURST'S HOUSE

Named after a giant or hobgoblin of pagan legends, Hob is a character found across the Peak District. He looked after the land and would ensure fertility of the farm in return for a bowl of cream. But if you angered him, by cutting down one of his trees or walling his land, he would wither crops and dry milk from the cows. So tread carefully when you visit Hob Hurst's House.

The 'house' is a very unusual burial mound. It is square instead of round, about 8 metres across, 1 metre high and is enclosed within a bank and ditch. Five small upright stones inside the top of the mound are what survive of a once larger stone setting. It is most likely about 4000 years old, though similar funerary mounds else-where in Britain were built less than 3000 years ago during the Iron Age. When Thomas Bateman excavated the mound in 1853 he found burnt human bones buried in a stone-lined grave along with two pieces of lead ore. Hob was probably not best please to find his house being dug into. Bateman only lived for another eight years, dying at the age of forty.

DIRECTIONS

Hob Hurst's House is on open access moorland above Harland Edge (SK287692). It can be reached by a footpath across Beeley Moor, beginning at a country lane over 2km to the east, or from a car park at Hell Bank Plantation to the south.

WET WITHENS

Wet Withens is one of the Peak District's largest ring cairns, and one of the most remote. There were originally eleven stones, seven of which are still standing, built on the inner edge of a continuous stone bank approximately 32m in diameter. There is no sign of an original entrance, which may have been blocked in prehistory as has been found at other ring cairns. The land drops away to the north, with the longest view across the Derwent Valley to the north east. The tallest stone of the circle is on the side facing this view. There is a small stone burial mound inside the circle.

The ring cairn is on moorland surrounded by prehistoric burial mounds, cairn fields and stone banks. One of the mounds has a stone covered in cup marks set in to its side.

DIRECTIONS

Wet Withens is on Eyam Moor (SK226790), and can sometimes be a challenge to find. It is 600m from the nearest entrance onto the moor, which is open access, but it's not served by any footpaths. The most obvious feature to look out for is the stone pile of a ruined shepherd's hut which is next to the ring cairn. The solitude and tranquillity is worth the walk for the more adventurous. The cup mark stone and barrow is at SK222786.

PIKE LOW BURIAL MOUND

Pike Low is a good example of a single burial mound built on a prominent hill. It overlooks Ladybower Reservoir but is only visible from nearby surrounding moorland. However, the hill itself dominates the valley below where flint tools have been found indicating farming contemporary with the burial between 4500 and 3500 years ago. There are also longer-distance views down the Derwent Valley to the south. Someone has excavated the mound in the past, leaving a deep hole, but not recorded their finds. Pike Low is one of 18 burial mounds in the Upper Derwent. Most are located on similar areas of the moorland overlooking the valley. These may have been associated with sheep pastures of families living below. One burial mound was built between the two distinctive outcrops of Crookhill, which are visible across the valley from Pike Low. Another three are found right down in the valley next to large concentrations of flint tools and waste flakes.

Pike Low burial mound can be seen silhouetted against the skyline from surrounding moorland.

DIRECTIONS

The mound (SK 181897) is a 2km walk from Fairholmes Visitor Centre, the second half of which is a steep climb onto rough heather moorland.

BEELEY MOOR

There are many burial mounds, stone circles and fields to be found on Beeley Moor near Chatsworth which show that the area was occupied throughout the Bronze Age. They cover an area of at least 3 kilometres with Hob Hurst's House at the northern end.

The highlight of the moor is an unusual triple stone cairn which is built just above the steep drop of Raven Tor. Three low stone mounds, each about 6 metres in diameter, are joined together to form an elaborate funerary monument. Each mound is built within a complete kerb of gritstone boulders. The kerb around the central mound is an impressive double row. The mound nearest to the edge may have been added later because its kerb overlaps the central cairn.

The three joined stone mounds on Beeley Moor look out north west towards the limestone plateau.

Part of the northern cairn's kerb is missing. This was removed when the site was used as a lead smelting hearth about 500 years ago; the prehistoric burial mound providing a convenient base for the leadworkers. It is amazing the cairn survives at all given the scale of later industrial activity in the area including stone quarrying as well as lead smelting.

There are other burial mounds in the vicinity around the triple cairn. There are further mounds, a stone circle and a ring cairn just over a kilometre to the north near Hell Bank Plantation.

DIRECTIONS
All of Beeley Moor's prehistoric sites are on open access moorland. The triple cairn (SK281 669) is best reached from the roadside to the north (SK290677). Cross the stile and follow the track onto the moorland then head south west straight towards Fallinge Edge. Once you reach the Edge follow it south until you come across the cairn. Other sites, including Hob Hurst's House can be readily explored from a small car park near Hell Bank Plantation (SK287681).

**NEW STONE AGE
(Neolithic)
TO EARLY BRONZE AGE**
4500 years ago –
3500 years ago
2500BC – 1500BC

Pyramids built in Egypt

POOLE'S CAVERN
See the entry for Poole's Cavern in Chapter 7.

CHAPTER 5
Settling Down

Much more evidence for settlement and farming survives from the Bronze and Iron Ages, between 4000 and 2000 years ago. Amounts of cereal pollen preserved in peat bogs increases during this period and the earliest dated field boundaries are about 3500 years old. Extensive areas of fields and the foundations of round buildings are found on the more favourable areas of the Eastern Moors. Elsewhere we find enclosed farmsteads and impressive hillforts. People were settling down more compared to earlier periods. They weren't necessarily living in the same place all year round or throughout their lives, but the range and frequency of movement appear to be less than the nomadic hunter-gatherers or first farmers. Two of the best understood settlements are Gardom's Edge and Mellor which have both been excavated as part of long-term archaeological projects.

Farming the Land

Small farming communities lived in timber round houses scattered amongst small, irregular fields. The fields form distinct groups that occupy relatively level shelves of lighter, sandy soils separated by heavier clay soils which were used as common pastures. They survive on moorland above medieval and later fields, occupying tracts of land not enclosed by more recent generations yet below altitudes prohibitive to prehistoric farmers. Elsewhere, later intensive cultivation and the growth of medieval villages have swept away the prehistoric fields, though fragments do survive where soils are too rocky for ploughing. We are lucky in the Peak District that the relatively low altitude of the Eastern Moors allows whole prehistoric landscapes to survive as mounds and linear piles of stone. They can be found if you walk on to the moorlands from the Derwent Valley and look amongst

Low-lying moorland such as this near Burbage Edge was occupied and farmed for at least 2000 years during the Bronze and Iron Ages.

the heather on almost any approximately level area of sandy ground above the top wall of the farmland.

Rocks had to be cleared from the thin soils to cultivate the land, and it is the result of this clearance that provides the most visible evidence for these prehistoric communities. Ancient field boundaries survive as earthen banks that formed against hedges or fences. Sometimes there are lines of stones that were dumped against these boundaries. Clusters of small clearance cairns dot the insides of these ancient fields. They are not always easy to see amongst heather unless the heather has been burnt for grouse shooting or archaeologists have excavated and reconstructed what they have found as at Gardom's Edge.

One of the surviving stone piles that was dumped here over 2000 years ago by farmers clearing the ground to cultivate crops.

A prehistoric field boundary being excavated on Eaglestone Flat. The boundary survives as a line of stones that were dropped against a hedge or fence possibly between 3000 and 4000 years ago.

The earliest dated agricultural features are banks of eroded soil trapped along field boundaries and clearance cairns. Examples have been radio-carbon dated to between 3700 and 3300 years ago on Big Moor and Eaglestone Flat, behind Froggatt Edge. These dates are roughly contemporary with burial mounds. The close association of fields with burials and stone circles suggests that fields across the Eastern Moors originated between 4500 and 3500 years ago.

Fields were cultivated with wooden spades and ards during the Bronze Age, with the introduction of steel-tipped ploughs only coming in the Iron Age. The study of pollen preserved in peat bogs shows that woodland was progressively cleared during the 2000-year period from the early Bronze Age onwards. Increasing amounts of cereal were grown in the fields, which were being more intensively cultivated during the Iron Age.

Most of the round houses were built of wood and measured between 8 and 11 metres in diameter. Timber posts supported walls of plastered hurdle fences and roofs

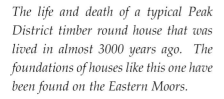

The life and death of a typical Peak District timber round house that was lived in almost 3000 years ago. The foundations of houses like this one have been found on the Eastern Moors.

thatched with straw, heather or rushes. Only two round houses are known with stone-footed walls, on Big Moor and Burbage Valley. Doors faced south east and the larger houses had elaborate wooden porches supported in deep foundations.

Pottery found at four excavated round houses, one on Big Moor and three on Gardom's Edge, is typical of that found on settlements dating from the later Bronze Age to early Iron Age. Two of the Gardom's houses have been radio-carbon dated to between 2600 and 2800 years old.

The fields surviving on moorland seem to have been abandoned by the end of the Iron Age as worsening weather and spreading blanket peat eventually made it impossible to cultivate the land. This was a long process as families tried to maintain their settlements with more favourable areas being occupied for longer. Areas at lower altitudes have probably been occupied from the Bronze Age to the modern day; it is just that the prehistoric settlements and fields have long been lost to subsequent cultivation and villages.

A round house being excavated on Gardom's Edge. The five people in the foreground are digging just in front of the door which survived as two lines of three deep holes that held the timber posts of a porch.

POLLEN CORES

You might think flower pollen, the bane of hayfever sufferers in spring and summer, is far too delicate to survive from prehistory. However, these tiny reproductive bodies have an almost indestructible outer shell that can survive for thousands of years in the right conditions. It is preserved best in peat bogs because of a lack of oxygen or in caves where cool temperatures and high humidity stop decay. Long cores can be taken from peat bogs and the pollen taken from the core for examination under a microscope. The lower down the core the pollen is found the older it is. Different plant families have different shapes and the types of plants surrounding the bog can then be identified and pin-pointed to different times in the past, especially when different parts of the core are radio-carbon dated. Archaeologists analyse the pollen to reconstruct the environment, including any cultivated plants such as cereals.

Defended from Attack?

At the same time as people were living in round houses amongst the fields, they were building impressive palisade fences and stone walls around some farmsteads and enclosing the summits of hills. There are 17 of these apparently defended sites in or around the Peak District, often referred to as hillforts.

The best surviving hilltop enclosures in the Peak are Mam Tor, Fin Cop, Castle Naze, Gardom's Edge and Carl Wark. Markland Grips in north-east Derbyshire and Wincobank in South Yorkshire are similarly impressive. There are even the remains of one having a good time at Alton Towers. At nearly all of these sites stone ramparts and deep ditches enclose large areas on the tops of hills or the corners of promontories. One of the most impressive is Mam Tor. Two stone ramparts crown the summit, enclosing dozens of platforms that once supported round buildings.

The top of Mam Tor is enclosed within two mighty stone ramparts and ditches. The dimples on the hillside are the platforms of prehistoric timber round houses.

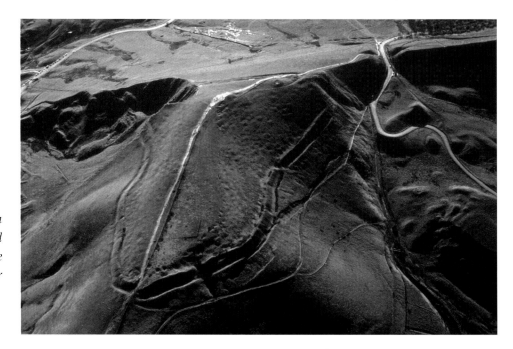

Three-thousand-year-old pottery, similar to that found at the round houses on Gardom's Edge, was discovered when the platforms were excavated. To date, Mam Tor is the only hillfort where buildings have been found.

The smaller sites look like settlements enclosed within stone ramparts or fences supported on earthen banks. They are about 100 metres across, or slightly less, and probably enclosed settlements of one or more buildings. The only two of these sites to be excavated are Ball Cross, overlooking the River Wye to the north east of Bakewell, and Mellor, crowning a hilltop above Stockport. At Ball Cross, a stone rampart was built behind a ditch. Pottery was similar to that found at Mam Tor and

A long bank of stones separates the top of Gardom's Edge from the remainder of the moorland. It was built about 3000 years ago only a short time before much of the moor was settled and farmed.

Castle Naze hillfort commands the high promontory on the northern end of Combs Moss near Buxton.

on Gardom's Edge, showing that Ball Cross was contemporary. The rampart was later pushed into the ditch. Mellor was a settlement of numerous round houses enclosed within a deep rock-cut ditch. It was occupied from the Iron Age, about 2500 years ago, to the end of the Roman period. On Tideswell Moor, Batham Gate Roman road cuts across one of the boundaries of an enclosed farmstead known as the Holmes which shows that it dates to before the Roman period.

All of these sites look like settlements that were defended from attack by raiders or cattle rustlers. But if so, why are there so many undefended settlements on the Eastern Moors of the same date as Mam Tor? The round houses scattered amongst the fields give the impression of a more peaceful society not feeling the need to hide behind high walls and fences. Violence was surely a part of later prehistoric life, but it probably took a very different form to the mass sieges envisioned by the Victorians who first coined the term hillfort. Warfare was probably small-scale and highly ritualised with forms of challenge and honour that required the correct response to a perceived slight. There may have been some raiding and feuding but this never involved large armies. The massive ramparts of Mam Tor would have been as much a symbol of community identity as a protective barrier. The occupants also knew that if raids did occur they were safe behind their walls – the nuclear deterrents of their day.

If we look closely at the enclosure on Gardom's Edge we can see that the boundary was never designed to be defensive. The wall was less than 1m high, contains a number of entrances and is built on relatively flat land. It has a boulder-strewn interior with little space for buildings and no evidence for settlement inside was found during the archaeological excavations. The Gardom's Edge enclosure has been radio-carbon dated to between 3400 and 2900 years old, only 100 to 600 years before the round houses in the nearby fields. There is also little room amongst boulders inside Carl Wark. If Carl Wark's builders had wanted to defend a settlement, they would have surely enclosed an area of flatter, boulder-free land just outside of its western rampart. There is also no water source inside to sustain people seeking refuge. Gardom's Edge and Carl Wark are more likely to have been ceremonial centres for people from the surrounding areas, a later revisiting of ideas about large-scale community gatherings in large arenas last seen in the New Stone Age henges.

WHEN'S A HILLFORT NOT A HILLFORT?

The mighty ramparts and impregnable locations of many Bronze and Iron Age hilltop enclosures led Victorian antiquarians to call them hillforts. They saw hordes of Celtic warriors besieging the walls of hillforts in much the same manner of nineteenth century armies. Later, archaeologists thought the hillforts would protect their occupants from raids during a period of continual warfare. Violence would have undoubtedly been a part of life in prehistory. But was it everyday and are all hilltop enclosures forts?

Hillforts vary immensely across Britain. Famous sites in Dorset such as Maiden Castle were massive settlements enclosed within ranks of two or more parallel ramparts. They are found close to each other in a densely settled landscape. However, there are as many unprotected settlements in the surrounding countryside as there are houses inside. You didn't need to live inside the hillforts suggesting that the level of violence wasn't so common that you were totally unsafe outside. Perhaps having a hillfort to run to for refuge was enough. There are equally densely settled areas without hillforts but plenty of suitable hills, such as the Yorkshire Wolds. Presumably they weren't settled by pacifists!

Archaeologists began to look more closely at hillforts in the 1990s and realised that they varied enormously between regions and from one hillfort to another. There were those which did enclose large settlements within high walls on well defended sites. Others had no evidence for occupation at all, or had only low walls never intended to be defensive. Some were actually built below higher land and could have easily been fired into from above. There is also very little evidence for hillforts actually being attacked. The famous Roman assault on Maiden Castle is an exception that involved a very different sort of enemy than had been present in the Iron Age. The Romans attacked Maiden Castle in huge numbers, a siege that the Victorians would have recognised, and easily overpowered the native defenders as a result. Iron Age warfare was probably much smaller in scale and less organised.

We now understand the complexity of hillforts. Some of those without houses were probably used for stock gathering, others for holding large communal ceremonies. Where hillforts were occupied, the ramparts certainly would have deterred others from attacking. But importantly they symbolised the community to others and may have been part of large-scale competitive display rather than everyday protection against raids. The building of the ramparts also brought the community together in shared labour that reinforced their social identity. You might want to think of hillforts and henges as football grounds, community centres and office parties all rolled into one.

Places to Visit

MAM TOR

The name Mam Tor means Mother Mountain, though the remains of ancient land-slides have also earned it the name Shivering Mountain. A massive landslip, caused by a bed of unstable shale, once collapsed from the east side of the hill causing the exposed rock face. The name suggests its central importance to communities living in and around the distinctive hogback hill. The hillfort occupies a spectacular location at the boundary between the gritstone and limestone, with the prominent hilltop being visible for miles. It dominates the western end of the Hope Valley and can be seen from many locations in the vicinity, including Carl Wark. The two lines

Mam Tor's ramparts seen from inside the hillfort. The grassed-over stone walls snake around the hill, rushes grow in the deeper soils filling the ditches behind the walls.

95

Mam Tor rises above the head of the Hope Valley. The prehistoric ramparts are so large they can be seen as lines ringing the hill from a distance.

of stone and timber ramparts that enclose the hill survive as grassed-over banks and ditches that can be seen as a dark line from the valley below.

If you approach Mam Tor from Mam Nick car park the bulk of the hill rises above you. You are walking towards the enclosure's southern entrance. The ramparts are at their most impressive here. The footpath takes you over the ramparts rather than in through the original entrance because of erosion but you can look down onto the entrance which is on your left. If you look to your right you can look along the double set of ramparts. Each bank is the grassed-over tumbled remains of a stone rampart with a silted-up ditch immediately behind it. The stone walls replaced earlier wooden palisade fences.

Follow the path onto the summit of the hill until you come to the Ordnance Survey's concrete trig pillar. The stone-flagged mound is a burial mound, now protected from erosion by the stones. A second burial mound is just below the summit near to the southern entrance. From here you can really take in the vast views of the gritstone moors and valleys and the limestone plateau. Edale is below you to the north and west, and Hope Valley stretches out to the east. This brings home how prominent the hilltop is – when it's not lost in cloud!

Continue along the footpath to the north east. If you look down the steep slope on your right you will begin to see some of the dozens of oval platforms that have been terraced into ground. These are the foundations of timber round houses. There is a spring behind the rampart overlooking Edale. The path takes you out through the hillfort's northern entrance.

Excavations in the 1960s identified how the ramparts were constructed and that the houses were approximately 3000 years old, dating from the end of the Bronze Age and beginning of the subsequent Iron Age. The remains of hearths and pottery were found in the house floors. It is unclear whether the ramparts are contemporary with the houses or built several generations later. The two burial mounds pre-date the enclosure by over 2000 years.

Archaeologists excavate the floor of one of the buildings on Mam Tor. Work in the 1960s suggested these were houses with hearths and broken pottery vessels.

Mam Tor (SK 127837) is situated approximately 2km west of Castleton where there is a visitor centre with displays about the history of the area. Access to Mam Tor is via a steep footpath from the National Trust's Mam Nick car park below its southern entrance. There is a small reconstruction drawing of what Mam Tor might have looked like on the way up. You can incorporate Mam Tor into a longer circular ridge walk from Castleton or Edale that either takes in Rushup Edge in one direction or Back Tor and Losehill in the other.

GARDOM'S EDGE

Extensive remains of prehistoric features dating from between 4000 and 2000 years ago are found on the moorland above Gardom's Edge. Rock art, houses, fields, burial mounds, a standing stone and the massive enclosure wall survive amongst the heather and birch woods. A number of the sites were excavated by archaeologists from the Peak District National Park Authority and the University of Sheffield in the 1990s. Parts of the enclosure, three round houses, an alignment of clay-filled pits, clearance cairns, burial mounds, the rock art and field boundaries were dug and restored for visitors to see.

Excavating one of the large stone mounds on Gardom's Edge. The mound began life as a formal monument about 4000 years ago then became a convenient dumping ground for stones cleared from a field over 1000 years later.

The enclosure is over 650 metres long. One side is defined by a stone rubble bank behind a façade of upright boulders. In one place, the bank may have replaced a line of timber posts and was widened by having burnt tree branches dumped against its inside which were covered with more stones. There are at least four entrances, each flanked by massive boulders and incorporating earthfast slabs as thresholds. The other side is the steep cliff of Gardom's Edge itself. The interior is strewn with boulders except for where it was later cleared for farming in the early Iron Age. It dates from about 3000 years ago and was probably a place for ceremonial gatherings rather than a hillfort.

The three round houses were timber-built, the largest being over 10 metres in diameter. Sherds of broken pottery and burnt cobbles from cooking fires were found outside the door of each house. Other finds include corn-grinding stones, shale bracelets and flint tools. The houses were ritually closed when abandoned. Corn-grinding stones were placed upside down in each building. One house had its doorway blocked with a low pile of stones that followed the curve of the wall, as if symbolically stating that the house could not be entered while it rotted away. Another house had more elaborate piles of stones built around its walls. A gap was left in front of the door which was subsequently narrowed and paved. Here, the location may have been re-used for another purpose once the building had decayed.

If you take the footpath that goes below Birchen Edge you will reach a corner of a field wall which is the end of the enclosed farmland. Walk approximately north west from here towards the birch trees and make for what looks like a pile of grit-stone boulders just before the woodland. This is one of the excavated round houses. You will see that the grass vegetation is much lower than the surrounding heather and exposes a reconstructed semi-circular stone bank. If you stand in the centre of the grassy area you are next to where the hearth kept the family warm about 3000 years ago. Look to the centre of the stone bank where there is a narrow gap – you are looking out of the house through where the original door once stood. The stone banks were added later, shortly after the house was abandoned.

An excavated round house is marked out by a ring of yellow flags. Each flag is in a hole that supported a wooden post or stake of the building's wall while the two red and white poles mark either side of the doorway.

The abstract rock art pecked into a large slab is one of the best examples in the Peak District. It can be difficult to find but is worth the search. Head west from the round house across the open ground towards another birch woodland growing above Gardom's Edge. As you get nearer to the trees look for a group of stone banks and mounds where the grass changes to heather. Amongst these is the low slab bearing the rock art. Further into the birch wood is a massive solitary standing stone over 3 metres high.

From the rock art skirt the birch woodland with the trees on your right towards the dry-stone wall that is the top wall of the farmland. Look out on your right for a long bank of stones. It is mostly vegetated over but closer to the wall you will find three areas excavated by archaeologists that are still free of grass and heather.

The distinctive prehistoric rock art on Gardom's Edge.

One of these is an entrance above two flat earthfast gritstone slabs. Near this entrance is a flat-topped stretch of bank with an outer face of large boulders.

Continue to the dry-stone wall and turn right along a path until you reach a ladder stile across another wall. Once you have crossed the stile look out for three small cairns built right above Gardom's Edge. These are called the Three Men and commemorate either shepherds who died in the snow or drunken priests who perished after losing their way. They are actually built on top of a wide, low burial mound, possibly an excarnation platform, that is at least 4000 years old. There are also magnificent views from the top of the edge across the Derwent Valley that take in parts of Chatsworth. The house is to your left and hidden from view but the Emperor fountain can be seen above the trees when it is flowing. On your way down you pass over the enclosure bank in the first grassy field, then you scramble down a short slope next to a large gritstone outcrop. The field in front of you takes you back down to the road. Look out for large stone cairns to either side which were piled up to clear another prehistoric field. About half-way to the road and on your right is a ring cairn on the edge of bracken.

DIRECTIONS
Gardom's Edge is situated on rough moorland just over 1km east of Baslow (SK273730). It is accessible along a steep 2km circular route beginning at the National Park car park, just off the Baslow to Chesterfield road. A good route is to turn left out of the car park, walk along the road a few metres until you see the footpath sign and take this path onto the moor below Birchen Edge. Return via the path above Gardom's Edge. The round house is located at SK275732, the rock art at SK274732 and the ring cairn at SK274724.

CASTLE NAZE

Mighty banks and ditches guard the northern promontory of Combs Moss, a swathe of high open moorland at nearly 450 metres above sea level.

Everything about Castle Naze is impressive. The most visible structures are two parallel walls separated by a ditch. Nearly 168 metres long, they run from cliff to cliff, dividing the promontory from the rest of the moorland to enclose an area of almost 1 hectare. The inner wall, built first, originally stood over 3 metres high and 10 metres wide at its base. A 17-metre-wide ditch was cut immediately outside of the wall, with a stone-faced bank added in front. An entrance punctures the centre of these ramparts.

Castle Naze. The end of the high promontory has been enclosed behind two massive stone ramparts and ditches.

Castle Naze has not been conclusively dated but is typical of Bronze and Iron Age hilltop enclosures dating from between 2000 and 3000 years old. The only dating evidence is a small amount of Roman pottery found just inside the wall. This may have been lost by native farmers living here or by Roman soldiers using the place as a watch tower.

DIRECTIONS

Castle Naze is situated on open access moorland 3km south of Chapel-en-le-Frith (SK053784). While it is only 200 metres from a road, the approach is up a steep climb suitable only for the fit!

BIG MOOR – SWINE STY

Prehistoric fields and settlements on Big Moor are found in close proximity to the Barbrook stone circles. Some of the mounds on the east side of the stream were funerary monuments, but many others were probably created as a result of clearing stones for agriculture. Fields on the west of the stream were enclosed within a network of boundaries on the flatter south east facing land. These were hedges or fences that had piles of cleared stone dumped against them and which trapped eroding soil. It is these stone and earthen banks that survive today – a sort of photographic negative of the original boundary. One of these banks has been radio-carbon dated to between 3700 and 3300 years old. This is how long ago a family was cultivating the adjacent land so causing soil erosion to form the bank.

Swine Sty is a settlement within the southernmost field on Big Moor. A stone-footed round house with a paved floor was excavated here in the 1960s by the Hunter Archaeological Society. It replaced a larger timber round house. The excavators founds prehistoric pottery dating settlement at the house to a 1000 year period between 4000 and 3000 years ago. They found lots of pieces of worked shale discarded during the craft-production of jewellery. The stone round house footings and the remains of the stone bank that formed a roughly square yard around the

The remains of prehistoric fields survive at Swine Sty as grassed over mounds amongst the bracken and heather. They show the hard work needed to clear the ground for farming.

house can be visited. Though the spot is fairly isolated today this would have been a busy place 3000 years ago. The house would have been warmed by a fire, sheep and cattle would have grazed in the fields nearby. The yard would have been occupied by people repairing tools, grinding corn and making clay pots. Some would be chipping away at lumps of shale to make the shapes of rings and bracelets that they later polished to create fine ornaments.

DIRECTIONS

Swine Sty and the fields on Big Moor make a good trip while visiting the Barbrook stone circles, if you can cross the steep sides of Burbage Brook (SK271750). Otherwise you can reach Swine Sty by crossing the open moorland from Curbar Gap car park. Look out for the green mounds poking above the heather and bracken. These are piles of cleared stone from fields. The house is not so easy to find but the remains of the stone wall around it can be discovered below a south-west-facing slope.

CARL WARK AND BURBAGE VALLEY

Burbage is Old English for the stream by the fortified place, an apt place name for the valley below Carl Wark. Over 230m long and 60m wide, Carl Wark is an impressive gritstone outcrop that rises out of the valley side. Its northern and eastern sides are sheer cliffs of bare rock, and the inside is strewn with boulders. The outcrop was enclosed sometime around 3000 years ago with a dry-stone wall of massive blocks along the southern side and a 3-metre-high rampart faced with more stone blocks. The walls mimic the circuit of cliffs that they complete. The entrance to the enclosure is in the southern wall. If you approach Carl Wark from the south and make towards the entrance you will be following in the footsteps of those people who made and visited the hillfort. The walls rise above the boulder-strewn slopes and turn inwards as they reach the entrance to create an impressive sight the closer you get. You can only reach the entrance after a steep scramble.

Carl Wark. The gritstone outcrop rises above Burbage Valley.

Once inside, turn around and take in the panorama that stretches down the Derwent Valley to the south. On a clear day the ring of trees encircling the Neolithic cham-

bered tomb on Minninglow breaks the horizon. Views in other directions are constrained by nearby moorland apart from to the west where you should be able to see Mam Tor, except that the rampart blocks sight of this other prominent hillfort. If you go to the northern end of the rampart, furthest from the entrance, you can get to the outside via the modern footpath. Look below you where the path passes the end of the rampart and you will see foundation blocks that took the rampart right to the edge of the cliff. The rampart is most impressive when seen from the outside where the effort and skills used to place the massive square boulders are best appreciated.

Most interpretations of the site believe it to be an early Iron Age hillfort, though Neolithic and early medieval dates have also been suggested. The boulder-strewn interior precludes extensive settlement of the sort seen at Mam Tor, while the lack of running water makes it unsuitable as a defensive refuge. The closest parallel in the Peak District is the Gardom's Edge enclosure which has been radio-carbon dated to the later Bronze Age, about 3000 years ago. Carl Wark is most likely to be the same date. An excavation in 1950 through the rampart was inconclusive.

Looking up towards the entrance and stone wall of Carl Wark hillfort. This is another so-called hillfort that was probably neither defensive or a settlement.

Two areas of prehistoric fields occupy free-draining sandy soils south of Carl Wark. One is an impressive group of over 70 clearance mounds with burial barrows and a ring cairn nearby. The heather-covered mounds can be seen clearly to either side of a footpath that passes through the centre of the area. The other, visible in a patch of burnt heather, has a long snaking rubble bank along its southern boundary and numerous small standing stones. The fields are either earlier or partly contemporary with Carl Wark.

DIRECTIONS
Carl Wark (SK259814) and the two areas of fields (SK253811 & 258808) are crossed by footpaths. The best approach is from the south, walking through one of the fields of clearance cairns and burial mounds before reaching Carl Wark via its original entrance.

MELLOR

Mellor was only discovered in 1995 when the owners of the houses neighbouring a field noticed how a strip of grass remained lush and green during the long, dry summer. Being fans of Time Team they suspected an archaeological feature and contacted the Greater Manchester Archaeological Unit. Within a couple of years they had full-scale excavations in the fields and their garden – and the Mellor Archaeological Trust was born. The archaeologists have been back every summer.

One of the most significant aspects of the site is a major Iron Age hilltop settlement enclosed within a large ditch excavated through bedrock down to the height of a person. A palisade fence followed just inside the line of the ditch. An almost

Excavating an Iron Age round house at Mellor with the reconstruction in the background of what a house from this period would have looked like. The edge of the house is visible as an arc of dark soil.

The deep inner ditch at Mellor which was cut through bedrock. The line of stones to the right of the ditch supported a palisade fence behind the ditch. The ditch is kept open and can be seen by visitors to Mellor.

complete Iron Age pot was buried in the ditch. Several timber round houses were protected by this ditch and palisade. Each was between 9 and 11 metres in diameter and was encircled by a specially dug drainage gully to carry away water dripping from the roof. As well as pottery, the excavators found pottery salt containers for transporting salt from the Cheshire Plains, a bronze-working crucible and slags from both bronze and iron working. Deposits in the bottom of the ditch were analysed for plant remains which indicated that the settlement was surrounded with mixed deciduous woodland and cereal fields.

Settlement continued throughout the whole of the Roman period, possibly by a relatively wealthy family. Pottery found here was made in Derbyshire, Cheshire, Lincolnshire and Samian came from central France. Finds of corn-grinding quern stones, loom weights and spindle whorls (used to spin wool) show that crops and animals were raised by the occupants living at Mellor. They continued to obtain salt from the Cheshire Plains.

The settlement is built on a very commanding location, occupying one end of a hilltop that has long-distance views across to the Cheshire Plain to the west. Many Iron Age settlements are found in such prominent locations, partly out of defence and partly as a way of signalling the community's right to live there to others in the surrounding area. The excavators originally thought that the view to the west indicated that this was a Roman military signal station but the nature of the finds is not typical of the Roman army and it was more likely a civilian settlement.

DIRECTIONS

Mellor is in the hills above Stockport (SJ981889). The excavations are centred around the church on the hill above the village. There is a public footpath overlooking part of the exposed ditch and a reconstructed roundhouse. You can see the archaeologists at work during an annual open day or get involved and join the digging team. Details of visits, participating and the finds to date are on the Mellor Archaeology website - www.mellorarchaeology.org.uk.

LATER BRONZE AGE TO IRON AGE
3500 YEARS AGO –
2000 YEARS AGO
1500BC – AD43

Trojan war and destruction of Troy

Rome founded

Great Wall of China begun

Maiden Castle and other hillforts are built

CHAPTER 6

Romans and Natives

It took the Roman legions just over ten years from the invasion of Britain in 43 AD before they built their first forts neighbouring the Peak District. The Romans didn't dominate the region straight away. At first, they encircled the hill country, building three forts next to rivers to the south, east and west. Two of these places would eventually become Derby and Chesterfield. A third was near Stoke-on-Trent. Was this the first contact between the power of Rome and the Peak District population? We'll never be sure, though news of Rome's overwhelming military victory over the southern tribes would have certainly preceded the arrival of the Romans themselves.

When the Romans Reached the Peak District

The earliest forts in the Peak District itself were built at Brough in the Hope Valley in 75 AD and at Melandra near Glossop in 78 AD. A third may have been built at Buxton, which became a bathing town called *Aquae Arnemetiae*, though the fort has not yet been found.

Brough and Melandra forts were called *Navio* and *Ardotalia* respectively by the Romans. These names appear on a later Roman road map of the Empire. They were typical auxiliary forts which housed cohorts of about 500 men drawn from Rome's provinces rather than legionaries. At both earth banks and timber palisades defended 1.2 hectares on promontories overlooking rivers. *Navio* was abandoned by the time Hadrian's Wall was built in 125 AD, perhaps because the new wall needed the men. According to a stone inscription, *Navio* was rebuilt and garrisoned in about 158 AD and remained in use until the fourth century AD. The later fort's defences were vastly more impressive, comprising a stone wall enclosed by up to

Archaeologists dig the vicus *beside Navio Roman fort.*

three wide ditches. *Ardotalia* was abandoned towards the end of the second century AD but unlike *Navio* it was never rebuilt. Perhaps *Navio* was needed to keep an eye on unruly locals or to help administer lead mining while *Ardotalia* was simply redundant in the now relatively peaceful province of Britannia.

The Romans built forts where they needed them to garrison newly acquired territory, placing each fort about a day's ride apart. They were usually next to rivers, which provided drinking water and an extra level of defence. The monumental size of the forts not only acted as defences, but also demonstrated the military power of Roman rule to surrounding native communities. They were ways of saying *you don't mess with us*. The materials needed to build the forts, initially large quantities of timber and subsequently stone for later rebuilds, were of course taken from the surrounding countryside. Communities would have no choice but to watch parts of their woodlands being felled by their new rulers.

Civilians weren't all kept at a distance from the forts. A small civilian village, known as a *vicus*, grew up outside nearly every major Roman fort. Both *Navio* and *Ardotalia* had one of these villages. Here lived civilians who followed the army to provide services but who were not allowed to live inside the forts. Metalworkers, blacksmiths, shopkeepers, even prostitutes would have lived there in small, timber buildings ranged along the roads and against the forts' defences. Partners and families of Roman soldiers also lived here. A Legionary or auxiliary soldier was not allowed to marry but that did not stop informal relationships developing. The original population of camp followers changed over time and with any re-deployment of the garrison. It is likely that local families quickly moved into the *vicus* when they saw opportunities to make a living dealing with the garrison. Roman rule slowly added a monetary economy to a one based around exchange and barter so that by the fourth century AD more of the population were using coins. Coinage had originally been reserved mostly for official transactions within the Roman state apparatus or as wealthy gifts to native leaders that were more high status objects rather than holding a monetary value. But over a period of 200 years much smaller denomination coins began to circulate and more inhabitants of Britannia used them to buy and sell goods.

Navio *Roman fort near Brough from the air. The outline of the fort is the square shape in the field at the centre of the photograph. The lines of its walls are marked by hedges and fences.*

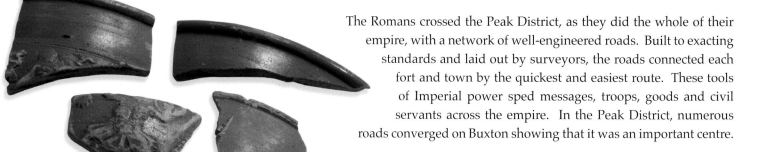

The Romans crossed the Peak District, as they did the whole of their empire, with a network of well-engineered roads. Built to exacting standards and laid out by surveyors, the roads connected each fort and town by the quickest and easiest route. These tools of Imperial power sped messages, troops, goods and civil servants across the empire. In the Peak District, numerous roads converged on Buxton showing that it was an important centre.

The Romans also introduced large-scale pottery production. Pottery had been little used during the previous 600 years when wood, leather and other organic materials had been preferred. Potters followed in the wake of the Romans to found kilns making wheel-thrown vessels near Derby in the second century AD. The type of pottery is known as Derbyshire ware and it became common for storage, transport and dining throughout the Peak District. It is found in almost all of the region's Romano-British rural settlements.

This Roman pottery known as Samian ware was manufactured in central Gaul and exported throughout the Empire. These sherds were found at Poole's Cavern, Buxton.

The Bath of Roman Peakland

Aquae Arnemetiae was the Roman name for Buxton. Like the modern town, it was centered on the natural hot and cold springs, and took its Latin name 'Aquae' from the waters. The Roman town was a bathing town, possibly in the vicinity of St Anne's Well. Most of the Roman town has long been lost under later development but some fragments were found during the building of the Crescent. Remains of a Roman bath-house, incorporating lead-lined baths and red painted wall plaster, were overlooked by a structure thought to be a classical temple. A hoard of 232 Roman coins and bronze jewellery was found during development work in the 1970s.

Wealth from the Ground

The Romans came to the Peak District as part of the general need to control their new province of Britannia. That might have been it except for what they found when they got here. Lead. An important metal that was bursting out of the limestone plateau's seams as galena ore. Veins were visible on the surface, had been worked since at least the Bronze Age, and gave the region a province-wide economic significance. Lead ingots inscribed with the word *Lutudarum* have been found across Britain with a concentration near Matlock. The name was listed in later Roman documents somewhere near Derby. Inscriptions suggest that lead production was undertaken by civilian contractors and companies rather than by the military. Small-scale lead-working has been identified at a number of settlements, including *Navio*, *Ardotalia*, Chee Tor and Carsington.

A Roman lead ingot found at Brough. It is inscribed in abbreviated Latin which says that it is lead from Lutudarum, Britannia.

Going Further Underground

A distinctive aspect of the Roman period in the Peak District was the use of caves. Roman objects have been found in at least thirty-three of the region's caves. Most common are coarse pottery such as Derbyshire ware, but there are also finewares, brooches, coins, tools, toilet instruments, iron weapons, lead weights, worked bone, whetstones and human burials. The most impressive assemblage is over 800 artefacts excavated in Poole's Cavern, near Buxton. There is also widespread evidence for the insertion of offerings, frequently in the form of coins or sherds of pottery, within chambered tombs and burial mounds.

One of the many Romano-British bronze brooches discovered at Poole's Cavern near Buxton.

The tendency for caves to be cold and humid, with poor removal of fire smoke makes them unlikely places for settlement except for short periods. Use of caves is not restricted to the Roman period, with deposits dating from throughout prehistory. Their marginal locations in the landscape, positioned as links between the world and underworld, may have made them attractive to different generations whether as places for burial, ceremonies or the transformation of raw materials into highly prized cultural objects. The caves tend to be close to Romano-British settlements, suggesting that these activities were undertaken by local communities.

Romano-British Farms and Villages

MULTICULTURAL ROMANO-BRITISH

Most of the people who lived in Roman Britain were not Roman. Most were British, with a cosmopolitan mix of people from all over the Empire. Britons came into greater contact with Roman ways of doing things, such as living in towns, building new styles of houses and using money. Some people chose to take on these new ways, while others resisted. British culture would have influenced the Romans also. Roman and British gods were often worshipped together, each religion influencing the other. In the centuries that Rome ruled Britain, later generations may not have thought of themselves as Roman or British but as Romano-British.

There many settlements and fields in the Peak District surviving from the Roman period. Some are small villages, such as Chee Tor and North Lees, while others are the sites of individual buildings scattered amongst fields. Building foundations show that a mixture of round and rectangular houses were built, the latter only introduced after the Roman invasion. This may suggest a change over time from traditional houses to new-fangled Roman style architecture, or differences in resisting and adopting the idea of Roman rule between members of any one community. Archaeological excavations at Chee Tor and Roystone Grange make these two of the best known Romano-British settlements in the Peak District.

These settlements would have mostly been occupied by 'Romano-British' people, a term used by archaeologists to show that they were a mix of native Britons and Roman settlers, both of whom were influenced by Roman society. A bronze plaque was found at Stannington on the eastern edge of the Peak District near Sheffield, which records the granting of citizenship to an infantry soldier upon discharge after twenty-five years service in 124 AD. The plaque was probably lost at the soldier's 'retirement' farm, given to him for his service. He had been recruited near the River Rhine, stationed at Caernarfon and retired in Sheffield!

Places to Visit

NAVIO

Navio was built in 75 AD on the southern side of the River Noe, using the river for protection from the north and as a reliable water supply. When it was rebuilt in 158 AD it was garrisoned with a unit drawn from Aquitaine, in south-west France.

The fort survives under grass as a rectangular raised platform, with more modern hedges following the lines of two of its walls. The fort and its adjacent *vicus* were excavated in the 1970s/1980s. At the centre of the fort was the headquarters, a stone building that housed the camp commander, and an open square. Barracks and other

If you approach the site of Navio *from Brough you will see this line of trees growing along a bank. This is actually the remains of the fort's eastern wall. Imagine a high stone wall and gate towers rising above you. The gate in the fence is right on the original entrance to the fort.*

buildings filled the remainder of the fort. The *vicus* was alongside roads leading to the southern and eastern gates. At least three roads ran from the fort's gates. One exited the northern gate towards the *Ardotalia* fort at Glossop. Two roads branched off just before the eastern gate; one towards a fort at Rotherham and another to the spa town at Buxton. This latter route is known as Batham Gate and is still followed by the road to Bradwell and Smalldale Street. A Roman bath house was found on the site of a thermal spring in Bradwell when the New Bath Inn was built on the road into Bradwell in the 1800s. This probably served the nearby garrison, though there is also the tantalising thought that a Romano-British settlement lies buried somewhere below Bradwell.

If you approach *Navio* along the footpath from Brough the first thing you will see is what appears to be a raised earthen bank on the horizon marked with a wire fence and a line of trees. You are looking at the fort's eastern wall. Imagine a solid stone wall at least twice your height with four strong towers; two at the corners and two in the centre. The central towers protected an imposing wooden gate about where the gate in the fence is today. Head towards this gate and you are almost walking

WAS *NAVIO* ATTACKED?

Archaeologists found a carved stone inscription dated 158 AD smashed and buried amongst debris dating from about forty years later. Does this point to an attack on *Navio*? The Empire was in turmoil at this time. *Septimius Severus* had taken control in Rome three years earlier. The Roman governor of Britain rebelled to claim power for himself. Forts across northern Britain were damaged and abandoned. Some were probably caught up in civil war as garrisons chose sides. Many units joined the governor's march on Rome. He was defeated in France by *Severus* who reclaimed Britain for the Empire. Somehow, *Navio* had been caught up in this imperial power play.

The remains of the strong room in the centre of Navio *fort. Winhill is in the background.*

along the line of the Roman road that ran to another fort in Rotherham. You are now walking through the location of part of the *vicus*. Either side of the road was fronted by wooden shops and workshops. The shop fronts were similar to covered verandas where goods and craft activities were displayed. Living quarters were to the rear of the buildings. The *vicus* would have been a awash with the noises of people haggling, of blacksmiths hammering red-hot iron, of cart wheels creaking over the sloping ground. Toxic lead-smelting fumes belched skywards. Soldiers would mingle with the civilians, buying things not provided for by the army or visiting partners and family not allowed inside the fort. You might even be propositioned by a prostitute. Depending on your business this would be a place to linger as you tried to sell your own goods or somewhere to hurry through on your way to the fort's commander. Or you might leave the road and pay a visit one of the altars dedicated to Hercules and local goddess Arnomecte.

Continue to the gate in the fence and you are about to enter the fort. It is worth making a detour to the left where the original stone wall is visible at the fort's corner. Once inside the fort continue walking towards the centre and you are following one of the original roads. About halfway across the field and to your left there is a low stone structure. This was part of a strong room that was inside the commander's headquarters, an impressive building of at least eight rooms arranged around a central courtyard. The headquarters overlooked the road. The rest of what is now the field on the platform was filled with regular rows of buildings that provided the accommodation, administration rooms and toilets of the garrison. There was a temple dedicated to Mars, god of war.

DIRECTIONS
The Roman fort is 200 metres north of the hamlet of Brough-on-Noe, 1km south east of Hope (SK 182828). It is accessible from a public footpath between Brough and Hope. Bradwell is only 1km to the south west.

ARDOTALIA

Ardotalia survives as impressive turfed banks and ditches on top of a promontory overlooking the River Etherow. The fort originally had a timber fence which was replaced with a 4-metre-high clay rampart reinforced with a stone wall. The original gateways survive as four breaks in the banks. There is one located in the centre of each side of the fort, which is typical of the layout of Roman forts. There were towers at each gateway and corner of the fort. The stone foundations of the headquarters buildings are visible near the centre of the fort. You can trace the walls and rooms that made up this once important military command centre. Little remains of other buildings, suggesting they were timber framed. There was a substantial group of buildings outside the fort. A *vicus* lay to the south east, now under houses, and a bath-house against the northern wall. There was also a 49-by 18-metre *mansio*, a post station, on the road leading to the fort's eastern gate.

Ardotalia was garrisoned by men from Frisia, the coastal region from north-western Netherlands across north-western Germany and into south-western Denmark, and Braca in Portugal. The Frisians were a Germanic tribe who spoke a language closely related to English.

The fort commands good views of the surrounding landscape which is dominated by the gritstone moorlands of the Dark Peak to the east.

*Ardotalia Roman fort near Glossop.
The fort survive as grassed over banks
punctured by the original entrances.
The commander's headquarters are
visible centre left.*

DIRECTIONS
Ardotalia, called Melandra on the Ordnance Survey, is situated on a low rise
south west of Hadfield (SK009951). It is easily reached by a public footpath
from the A57 or by parking just to the north of neighbouring Gamesley.

*The view to the east from Ardotalia
Roman fort. The fort commanded a
route that crossed the Peak District
from west to east.*

The impressive Romano-British field boundaries of Chee Tor were formed as a result of ploughing eroding soil down the slope where it became trapped behind the original walls or hedges.

CHEE TOR

One of the best preserved Romano-British villages in the Peak District is located on the steep-sided promontory of Chee Tor. The ground drops dramatically down into Chee Dale on all sides except to the south east where the land gently rises towards the medieval village of Blackwell. At first glance this might appear to be a good defensive location. However, it was more likely chosen because the people who settled here chose the thin soils of the rocky outcrop to keep the deeper soils to the south for agriculture.

You can see the regular pattern of ruined limestone walls that form yards and streets of the village. The yards neighbour each other and some would have contained houses and other buildings. Levelled areas suitable for buildings are clearly visible in some of the yards. Neighbours were very close to each other at Chee Tor, but they built fences supported on the low walls between each other. You can wander from one yard to another and along the original village lanes visualising the Romano-British buildings clustered around you. This village would have been a hive of activity and noise, as people came and went between the village and its fields to the south and east. The streets weren't paved so they probably churned up into mud during wet weather.

Archaeological excavations were conducted here in the 1970s by Harry Lane. He discovered pottery dating from the second to fourth centuries AD, most of which was Derbyshire ware made in the kilns near Derby. A burial was also found just outside the village in a simple grave. There was also evidence for small-scale lead working. A geophysical survey of the village, which picks up features still buried below ground, indicated lots of burnt material lay beside some of the yard walls. This may be the result of families throwing waste from their house hearths against the walls.

An impressive group of regularly-laid-out earthworks survive on a steep slope 500 metres to the east of the village. These are long earthen banks, all that remain of field boundaries that have long disappeared. The earthworks were created as soil was eroded downslope during ploughing and became trapped against the boundaries. The original boundaries might have been stone walls, now buried below ground, or hedges. They form a regular pattern of square and rectangular fields that are best seen from the Miller's Dale to Wormhill road on the opposite side of the dale. The fields only survive because this area is too steep to have been ploughed since Roman times. Blackwell's medieval open field covered all the deeper soils on the gentler land to the south of Chee Tor and its fields. Romano-British fields probably covered much the same area but have been destroyed by medieval ploughing.

DIRECTIONS

A right of way passes through Chee Tor between Blackwell Hall and the old railway station in Miller's Dale, now on the line of the Monsal Trail (SK126732). It is a steep climb up from Miller's Dale. The nearest car park and public toilets are at the station.

ROYSTONE GRANGE

Roystone Grange is a valley with a long history etched into its landscape. From the Bronze Age to the Industrial Revolution, people have come here to work the land. We know a lot about life in the Roman period because of work carried out by local farmer Martin Wildgoose and the University of Sheffield.

One or more families lived here in the second and third centuries AD, occupying a small group of timber buildings in the valley. At least two buildings were constructed on large boulder-revetted terraces. One of these can be seen from the footpath next to

The foundation platform of one of the Romano-British houses at Roystone Grange. Short timber posts mark the post holes found by archaeologists that held posts to support the roof. The snaking wall in the distance follows the line of one of the original Romano-British farm boundaries.

The Roystone Grange valley was farmed during the Roman period. Two-thousand year-old building platforms and the lower courses of field walls survive to show how the land was occupied.

the large dairy building. This and another house nearby were excavated in the 1970s and 1980s. They both had rectangular floor plans with rounded gable ends and roofs supported on two rows of timber posts. The floors were paved with limestone slabs. One house had a walled and cobbled yard attached. Most pottery found in the buildings was storage vessels made in the kilns near Derby, though there were also pots from further south. One was a piece of a second century AD Samian ware, a type of mass-produced pottery made in central France that was exported throughout the Roman Empire. One of the buildings was rebuilt on the same location to a smaller size in the third century AD. Both may have still been occupied 100 years later.

The occupants of the buildings farmed an estate that comprised two large fields on opposite hills either side of the valley. The boundaries of these two fields still survive, having been incorporated into the later pattern of fields. Their lines can be picked out on maps and aerial photographs, from which they have been compared to the wings of a butterfly. The walls were built in a characteristic Romano-British style. Two parallel rows of large limestone boulders were laid on the ground and the space in between filled with rubble to form a high wall. If you look closely at the walls around Roystone Grange you will see that some of the current field walls are built on top of the surviving Romano-British boulders. Small layered stones typical of eighteenth century enclosure walls sit on top of Romano-British foundations which means that these boundaries have remained in use for almost 2,000 years. One wing of the butterfly is now the open access area called Roystone Rocks. The other, to the south east, was subdivided into a very regular pattern of rectangular fields in the eighteenth century.

The remains of at least six parallel stone banks can be seen climbing up the west-facing slopes of this second big field. They are clearest where they have been cut by a grassy track. In low light you can make out low, narrow ridges between the banks. These are 'lazy beds' which were created to deepen the soil for spade cultivation. The stone banks demarcated different people's plots of land and helped to clear the thin ground of stones. Excavations in this area confirmed that these banks date to the Romano-British period.

Roystone Grange has a very remote feel to it today, hemmed in as it is by two hills. The valley is narrow and winding and doesn't seem on first impressions to be a great place for a settlement.

DIRECTIONS

To reach Romano-British Roystone Grange (SK200569) follow a 10km easy-going heritage trail from Minninglow car park. The north-west butterfly wing and part of the other are open access land. A self-guided trail leaflet with information about each site is available from Bakewell Visitor Centre on online at www.peak-experience.org.uk. You pass a Neolithic tomb, medieval monastic grange, and later industrial archaeology. There is an information board on the barn next to the Romano-British building platforms, as well as other boards pointing out the later history of the Grange.

NORTH LEES

The remains of a small Romano-British village survive near North Lees Hall, Hathersage. It is located on a gently south-west-facing valley side near to springs that feed into Hood Brook. Stanage Edge towers overhead to the north while the Derwent Valley is to the south. Steep land rises on all sides except for down the brook to the south. This gives the location a slightly remote feel, the settlement occupying its own small valley.

The village is laid down the slope as a series of clearly visible long terraces built one above the other. Each is about 20 metres long and no more than 5 metres wide. Low stone walls, some constructed of massive gritstone boulders, support each terrace. Each terrace supported one or two buildings, and the square platforms for some of these can still be seen in places. It is unknown whether a terrace was occupied by a single family, perhaps with a house and an outbuilding, or whether the houses of more than one family huddled next to each other. About half way down the village are the remains of a circular walled enclosure built of large stone blocks. The wall is under 1 metre high and probably supported a timber palisade or turf wall. Part of its wall is now crossed by the later field wall that separates the archaeological site from fields to the south. This structure is totally different to the terraces. The difference may be because of a number of reasons. It may have had a different use such as a livestock pound; however, its flat interior suggests that there was also a house or other building here. It looks like one family had enclosed their building within some form of boundary. This could have been constructed before or after the rest of the village or be to do with the different social status of the people who lived in the enclosure.

A small archaeological excavation into one of the terraces found Romano-British pottery, mostly Derbyshire ware, and a corn-grinding quern stone. The stone indicates that cereals were grown and made into flour by the people who lived in the village.

The amount of work needed to make the terraces in the first place was significant. Were they all constructed at the same time as a communal building project or did the village grow more organically over time with another terrace added when needed? We have the builders' choice of ground to thank for their survival. They decided to build their houses on a rocky outcrop which has not since been ploughed. This was probably a deliberate choice to seek out agriculturally unproductive land with stones for the terraces readily at hand. Fields were on the deeper soils of the adjacent improved farmland, between the village and the remains of the old chapel. The field boundaries have been largely ploughed out but faint traces can still be seen if the sun is low and the gentle banks cast slight shadows across the pasture. There appears to have been a large oval field which was subdivided into rectangular plots.

These gritstone boulders retain the edge of a long terrace at North Lees near Hathersage. The terrace supported the buildings of a Romano-British village.

The large stone on the left marks the end of a Romano-British terrace at North Lees. The upright stones to its right follow the front of the terrace. Stone lines of further terraces below can be seen in the distance.

It is worth exploring each of the village terraces in turn, taking time to think what it would have like to live here almost 2000 years ago. Your home is surrounded by others, their clay daub walls and thatch roofs somewhat reminiscent of Central American adobe houses. Corn is ripening in the adjacent fields and someone is grinding some of last year's harvest into flour using a circular corn-grinding quern, rotating one heavy gritstone on top of another. Sheep are pastured on the moorland grazing above, cattle on the lower land.

DIRECTIONS

The Romano-British village is crossed by a public footpath that runs beside a woodland north of North Lees Hall (SK235837). The Hall is also noteworthy. This was the model for Mr Rochester's Thornfield Hall in Jane Eyre. Charlotte Bronte visited Hathersage for a few months prior to writing her novel and she visited the Hall which was owned by the Eyre family.

POOLE'S CAVERN

Poole's Cavern is a natural limestone cave that formed over two million years ago. Archaeological discoveries were first made when the cavern became a showcave in 1853. Human and animals bones were found when deposits of glacial sediments were dug out of the entrance to improve access. Further excavations were undertaken in 1865 and 1890, followed by a more extensive dig in the 1980s.

The results of these excavations show that the cave was used from the New Stone Age to the Roman period. Prehistoric pottery was discovered inside the cave while polished stone axes and flint tools dating from about 4500 to 3500 years ago are relatively common outside. The axes were quarried in Cornwall and Cumbria. There is a 4000 year old burial mound on Grinlow, above the cavern, where several crouched human skeletons and a cremation were found during late-nineteenth-century excavations. One burial was accompanied by a decorated Food Vessel placed near the body's hands. Flints and animal bones were also discovered in the graves.

The vast majority of evidence for use of the cave dates to the Romano-British period. The cave was used as an important metal smithing workshop during the second century AD, probably by people living outside the cave. Large numbers of jewellery items were produced here as evidenced by surviving objects. These included a range of enamelled, trumpet and disk brooches, earrings, finger rings and studs made in bronze, iron and lead. An iron knife and a lead weight were also discovered. Evidence that these were made inside the cave includes a small crucible, molten blobs of bronze, hammered bronze ingots and sheets and part-smelted lead ore. A bronze brooch still had untrimmed flashing attached from the casting process. There were also lead mould formers, the blanks used to make the clay moulds, for brooches and other jewellery items.

A large quantity of contemporary pottery was found alongside the metalworking remains, including decorated Samian ware from central France and large storage jars known as amphorae. Other finds included bone pins and utensil handles. There was an abundance of food waste; cattle, sheep and pig bones and teeth, bones of brownhare, domestic fowl and fish, and shells of oysters and cockles. Adding to

Inside Poole's Cavern, Buxton. The cavern was occupied from the Neolithic to the Roman period.

Excavations inside Poole's cavern have found archaeological evidence for over 4000 years of human activity including hundreds of Romano-British bronze jewellery items. The cavern appears to have been a major metalworking workshop during the Roman period.

One of the pieces of Roman jewellery found in Poole's Cavern.

ROMAN OCCUPATION OF BRITAIN
2000 YEARS AGO – 1600 YEARS AGO
43AD – 400AD

Roman invasion of Britain 43AD

Coliseum built in Rome

Byzantine Empire founded at Constantinople

the large assemblage were at least 19 Roman coins. There were also at least six human burials.

Why was the cave used for metalworking? Suggestions have ranged from the comparative seclusion of the cave to its stable year-round temperature and humidity. Caves may offer some security for storing valuable materials and finished products. Also of importance is the fact that metalworking is an important transformation of natural materials into cultural objects, and jewellery is highly prized at that. This is not just a practical process but an act that held high social significance. Perhaps the cave was chosen because it was itself an important location suitable for this sort of work to be undertaken, a link between the underworld and the everyday world. This could explain the burials and the use of the cave since the New Stone Age.

Poole's Cavern has been a popular tourist destination ever since Charles Cotton wrote it up as one of the 'Seven Wonders of the Peak' in the 1680s. Visitors were shown around the cave by local cottagers during the eighteenth and early nineteenth centuries. The guides would often threaten to extinguish their candles unless they were paid more while visitors often threw stones at the stalactites and stalagmites. The showcave was opened in 1853 by the cavern's owner, the Duke of Devonshire. Visit the Poole's Cavern website for further details including opening times - www.poolescavern.co.uk.

DIRECTIONS
Poole's Cavern is located in Buxton Country Park which is to the south west of Buxton. Many of the finds are on display in the Cavern's Visitor Centre and at Buxton Museum. There is a footpath through the park to Grinlow which now has a stone tower on top of it called Solomon's Tower.

MELLOR
See the Mellor entry in Chapter 6.

CHAPTER 7
Illuminating the Dark Ages

The Peak District, like many areas of Britain, goes quiet at the end of the Roman period. We have few archaeological sites that tell us what happened to people and the landscape in the next two or three centuries. The pace begins to pick up again about 300 years later, in the 700s AD. We begin to see large territorial boundaries, local nobles being buried in richly-furnished graves, Britons, Anglo-Saxons and Vikings vying with each other for land. It is also the time when the 'People of the Peak' are recorded in an early tax document.

The shafts of carved stone crosses are one of the most visible reminders of early medieval society in the Peak District.

Decline and Fall?

To archaeologists today, it is as if whole generations disappeared at the end of the Roman Empire – the dark ages after the light of civilization! But people continued to live in Britain during this period. So why are they so invisible? This is partly because the pottery kilns stopped production, so making the sites of houses difficult to find and date. The end of the Roman Empire was a complex and long drawn out affair that had many reasons for decline and an equally large number of repercussions. There is perhaps one main reason why the kilns stopped. The economy suffered greatly from the withdrawal of the Empire – suddenly the whole economy of taxes and wages for those working in the Roman government was removed. Without a large standing army and body of civil servants to keep in food, clothes and other goods, families who made these goods or raised crops and livestock saw their incomes disappear. With little money to spend on the sorts of foods stored and transported in the pottery vessels, they slowly returned to producing enough food for themselves. Wood, skin or wicker became the commonest, in some places, only materials to make vessels and plates from again – not that they had been abandoned

The Grey Ditch is picked out by its shadow where it runs downslope above Bradwell. The impressive earthwork runs across a valley that gave access between the limestone plateau and Hope Valley, and may have been built after the end of the Roman Empire.

during the Roman period. Because these easily rot unless preserved under favourable conditions, the ability of archaeologists to identify and date settlements is very difficult. One site that may survive from the post-Roman turmoil is the Grey Ditch, a massive earthen boundary that crosses a valley near Bradwell.

People of the Peak

By 700 AD the Peak District lay on the border between two rival Anglo-Saxon kingdoms – Mercia to the south and Northumbria to the north. It is then that the name 'Peak District' originates. It derives from the Mercian name for the occupants of the region, the Pecsaetna which means Peak Dwellers. This name is first used in a document sometime around 700 AD to refer to 1200 families who paid tax to the Mercian king. The document doesn't give a specific description of where this group of people lived so we don't know whether it refers to the whole of the Peak District or just one part. Nor does it mean that the people who lived here saw themselves as one unified community or tribe. It may simply be a convenient tax collecting district for the Mercian king, a way of grouping all the people who lived in those hills to the north. Whichever was the case, the name Peak stuck when describing the southern part of the Pennines so that today most of the region is the Peak District National Park and the geology is divided between the Dark Peak and the White Peak.

Between Kingdoms

Also about this time individuals were once more buried in mounds. At least 38 early Anglian burials are found across the south of the region, many made within existing prehistoric mounds. They are accompanied with grave goods. Most are everyday items, such as knives, but nearly half of the burials contain much more special objects, including swords, jewellery and semi-precious stones. Burials with fancier goods are probably those of local rulers. One of the most spectacular discoveries was a richly furnished grave at Benty Grange that included the rare find of an

Anglian helmet. Another well investigated burial is that of Wigber Low where at least five burials were made into an already ancient Bronze Age cairn. Anglian grave goods in the Peak District are all typical of objects found across Mercia and suggest a great deal of contact with the Midlands. This and the tax document show that the Mercian kingdom had a great deal of influence on part of the Peak District. The absence of the burials in the north of the Peak District may be important. Was there a different group of people living there without Mercian affiliations?

An Anglian burial mound under excavation. Finds from these burials suggest local leaders connected with the Mercian kingdom to the south. This does not necessarily mean the dead were Anglo-Saxon; they could equally have been the descendents of Romano-British families who identified themselves with the new political powers.

How do you make a Viking cross?

Not difficult given the reputation of your average Viking! Viking nobles were one group of people who erected carved stone crosses in the Peak District. Crosses dating from 600 to 1000 AD are found in many villages.

Christian missionaries had started to visit the Peak District in the 600s AD when Christianity was only beginning to replace indigenous Anglo-Saxon religion. A Northumbrian saint, Betti, visited the south-east part of the Peak around Carsington where he erected a small cross to preach from. It now stands on the Carsington village green where it was moved from the grounds of Hopton Hall. Alstonefield was visited by the Northumbrian Saint Oswald, Bishop of York, in 892 AD. He paid a visit to combat a revival in local pagan worship and founded the church to impress the power of the Church on the locals.

Crosses were carved under the patronage of local lords as displays of their authority and status, who provided the crosses as places for people to hear preachers and celebrate mass. Differences in styles of knotwork and other decoration have been interpreted as indicating different time periods or the ethnic group of the person having the cross made. One archaeologist suggests that some crosses are typical of Mercian decoration, some Northumbrian and the others Scandinavian. If so, the crosses demonstrate something of the ethnic mix of those living in the Peak District over 1000 years ago. Beautifully carved cross shafts survive in the churchyards at Bakewell, Bradbourne, Eyam and Hope.

Above left: *Eyam cross is one of the best preserved early medieval stone crosses in the Peak District.*

Above middle: *Intricate knotwork is another common early medieval decoration found on stone cross shafts.*

Above right: *Ornate carved designs on cross shafts include curling vine scrolls such as these at Bradbourne which are highlighted by lichen growth.*

Scandinavian families had become more prominent sometime after 900 AD when the Peak District lay on the western boundary of the Danelaw, a vast area covering the East Midlands and Yorkshire. Northumbria also became more influential during the same century. Thus the Peak District lay on the borders of the two competing kingdoms of Mercia and Northumbria and between the Anglo-Saxon and Scandinavian dominated political regions. Then, in 924 AD came a decisive moment in the shaping of modern England and Scotland. Edward the Elder of Wessex fought with his northern neighbours until they accepted his rule. The kings of Bernician Northumbria, Viking Northumbria, Strathclyde and Scotland met to sign a treaty with King Edward at Bakewell. Edward reputedly built a fortification, known as a burh and the origin of the word borough, for the occasion and was declared ruler of all the Britons.

The location of Edward's burh at Bakewell has long remained a mystery, no one really knowing whether the fortified site has survived to the modern day. The burh would have been a square piece of land enclosed within a bank and ditch. The defences could have easily been lost below Bakewell's streets and buildings as the town grew from the medieval period onwards. The exact location of the burh remains a mystery to this day. It was long thought to have been on the aptly

132

named Castle Hill but no evidence has ever been found there. A local archaeologist has recently suggested earthen banks next to the River Wye that form the boundaries of existing fields have their origins in the burh's defences. The feature remains undated.

Life Goes On

But what does this all mean for those actually living in the region? Were they continually threatened by new warlike invaders, Britons, Saxons and Vikings replacing each other after another bloody battle? Or were different ethnic groups jostling with each other for room to live and farm, perhaps with the later arrivals fitting around the existing populations? We're unlikely ever to know. There are no dated settlements of this period of great change. Place-names suggest a multiethnic society. Some show locations where British communities may have continued to live and work the land, others where Anglo-Saxon and Scandinavian populations settled. DNA testing can indicate someone's genetic make-up but not how they thought of themselves or which social group they identified with. The types of artefacts found in the burial mounds only tell us what objects the mourners chose to place in the graves, not the ethnic identity of the dead. Anglo-Saxon metalwork and designs could just as easily have been owned by communities descended from Britons as Anglo-Saxons. What the objects tell us is which greater political entities those families identified themselves with rather than what their DNA contained. The Peak District, like all of Britain, was very much a multicultural place on the eve of the Norman Conquest in 1066 AD.

A decorated bronze escutcheon from an Anglo-Saxon hanging bowl found during excavations at Roystone Grange. The design combines spirals with stylised animal heads. It was found in a later medieval farmhouse so may have been found by the farmer and kept as an heirloom.

Sites to Visit

GREY DITCH

Grey Ditch is possibly one of the earliest monuments built following the Roman withdrawal from the Peak District. The ditch is actually an earth bank with a ditch along its northern side built across the road south from *Navio*. It runs across

Excavations indicate what a formidable barrier the Grey Ditch was. Little dating evidence was found except for a single piece of Roman pottery underneath the bank.

Bradwell Dale just to the north of Bradwell village, joining two precipitous ridges. It seems to protect this easy access route on to the limestone plateau from the north, but we still don't know who built it or when. Recent excavations found Roman pottery in the soil beneath, which shows that Grey Ditch was later than the Roman period but does not give an exact date.

It could have been built any time from the late Roman to the early medieval periods. The ditch was regularly cleaned out, showing that it was repeatedly visited to maintain it as a significant feature in the landscape. Locating the ditch on the northern side suggests it was built by people living on the plateau to differentiate them from others living in the Hope Valley to the north. It has been speculated that it may have been built by Anglian communities on the plateau to separate themselves from Britons to the north but we will never know its precise use until it is better dated and understood.

DIRECTIONS

Grey Ditch is just outside the village of Bradwell (SK177805). It is easily visited by public footpath from the centre of Bradwell, and could make part of a longer walk that includes *Navio* and Hope.

The Grey Ditch was actually a massive bank and ditch that defended the north-south route along Bradwell Dale.

HOPE

Hope was a major Anglo-Saxon administrative centre in the Peak District. It was first recorded in an Anglian chater in 926 AD which referred to Hope as one region with Bakewell and Ashford. All three places were obtained from a Scandinavian lord by King Athelstan of Wessex after he won a battle nearby.

By the time Hope was recorded in the Norman Domesday Book in 1086 it was the heart of a large estate that covered much of the High Peak and probably home to a Saxon 'earl'. It was this estate that probably formed the basis for the Norman's Royal Forest of the Peak after the Conquest of 1066 AD. The estate included Edale, Aston, Shatton, Tideswell and part of Offerton.

Hope was recorded in the Domesday as having 30 villagers, a priest, church, mill and land for 10 ploughs. It was the King William's own land and his son William Peveral was in charge who lived nearby in the delightfully named Peak's Arse – now Castleton. The original Saxon church was replaced first by Norman stonework and the building is now all later medieval. A good example of a Norman arch can be found inside Castleton church. Next to the church is a large mound that was either a 'motte' which supported the Norman castle or a 'moot' where Saxon landowners met to debate. There are three stone cross shafts inside the churchyard. Two are plain and worn stumps, but one is carved with beautiful and intricate designs carved in relief. The cross itself has long gone. The east and west faces both contain elaborate knotwork that frames two figures. The figures appear to be fighting or embracing on the west face while the pair on the east face are standing either side of a tree. There is also a flower or leaf motif on the east face and two intertwined snakes on the north face. The cross is similar to one of the two crosses in Bakewell churchyard.

The ornately decorated cross shaft at Hope which depicts human figures fighting or embracing on one side and standing either side of a tree on the other.

DIRECTIONS
The church is at the eastern approach to the village (SK173835).

EYAM

Eyam is a rare example of a surviving cross head. Three angles with trumpets play a fanfare for the seated angel in the centre.

Famous for the plague of 1666 that wiped out most of its villagers, Eyam has a much longer history. The name is derived from Old English and means place between streams, referring to its location next to springs. Eyam was recorded in the Norman Domesday of 1086 AD when it had 12 villagers and 7 smallholders. No church is mentioned at that date.

Inside the churchyard stands one of the best preserved Anglo-Viking crosses in the Peak District. Over 2 metres high, the shaft is ornately carved in relief. The west and east faces contain scrollwork depicting curling vines and leaves while the other two sides are decorated with knotwork. Similar vines are found on one of the crosses at Bakewell. There is also a carving of a person holding a trumpet or horn which may be a prophet or Christ, and above this what may be the Virgin Mary. The cross has four scenes on either side depicting three angels blowing trumpets or holding staffs arranged around a central seated angel. The original cross was much taller as indicated by a slight mis-match in sizes between it and the top of the shaft which shows that a piece of the shaft is missing. The cross was once a wayside preaching cross to the west of the village and was moved to the churchyard after the plague.

DIRECTIONS

The church is in the centre of the village (SK218764).

BENTY GRANGE ANGLO-SAXON BURIAL

'…when the patterned blade of a hammer-forged sword, stained with blood, mighty of edge, shears through the boar-crest above opposing helmets.'

When the antiquarian Thomas Bateman excavated a burial mound at Benty Grange Farm on the 3rd of May 1848 he was probably expecting to find another prehistoric urn cremation. Instead, he discovered one of the richest Anglo-Saxon burials in the Peak District.

There is little to see of the burial site today which is on private land, however the finds are on display at Weston Park Museum, Sheffield. Buried with the deceased were a warrior's helmet reminiscent of descriptions in the Saxon saga *Beowulf*, metal hanging bowls and a wooden cup decorated with metal designs. These were the grave goods chosen by the mourners to honour a wealthy individual during the person's funeral. This was probably sometime after 600 AD. The helmet and cup were decorated with crosses, showing that the person or his grieving family were Christian. At least one Northumbrian missionary, Saint Betti, visited the Peak, and others may have come from recently converted Mercia.

The helmet is the most impressive find. It survived as a framework of iron bands with a nose guard and a bronze boar forming a crest. It is one of only four Anglo-Saxon helmets ever found in England, including those at York and Sutton Hoo. Boar crested helmets are mentioned in Anglo-Saxon sagas. *Beowulf* refers to boars protecting the wearer from sword blows.

Nearly 140 years after its excavation, a replica of the helmet was made for Weston Park Museum, Sheffield in 1986. It is on display next to the original.

A reconstruction of the spectacular find of an Anglo-Saxon helmet from Benty Grange. The helmet is one of only four found from this period in England. The boar crest was thought to help protect the wearer from sword blows.

DIRECTIONS
Weston Park Museum is located in the park of the same name to the north west of Sheffield city centre. The Benty Grange helmet is one of many finds from ancient Peak District that are displayed and interpreted in the museum.

ALSTONEFIELD AND ILAM
There are Saxon architecture and artwork in the churches of these neighbouring villages. Parts of Alstonefield's original church still survive, incorporated into later medieval rebuilds of its distinctive red and grey walls. The colours come from the two types of stone used in the walls – pinky red sandstone and grey white lime-stone. Inside, the eight-sided stone font bowl and a coffin also date from the time the Northumbrian Saint Oswald visited Alstonefield. The font was rediscovered

The Saxon font at Ilam church is ornately carved with men and dragons that depict scenes from the life of St Bertram, a converted Mercian king.

when it was dug up from the churchyard. Fragments of crosses carved with knotwork designs are built into the wall near the porch. There is one short part of a shaft standing in the churchyard. Some of these may have been commissioned by Saint Oswald himself as wayside preaching crosses for erection around the parish.

Ilam church contains another Saxon font, ornately carved with men and dragons that reputedly depict scenes from the life of St Bertram. Bertam was an eighth century Mercian king who visited Ireland to study Christianity where he met a beautiful princess and took her back to Mercia. Sometime later she and their son were killed by wolves and Bertram sought a life of prayer, converting many pagans by example. That's why he's a saint.

DIRECTIONS

Alstonefield church is 200m south-east of the village (SK133554). Ilam is 4km south of Alstonefield and the church is to the south east of the village (SK133507).

BAKEWELL CROSSES

There are two Anglo-Viking crosses in Bakewell churchyard, both carved with intricate relief patterns. One has human figures, including a horse rider, on the surviving piece of its cross as well as a beautifully depicted horse on the top of the shaft. The rest of the shaft is decorated with vine scrolls and leaves similar to those on the Eyam cross. The other has lost its cross, only the shaft remains, which is covered in knotwork designs similar to those on the Hope cross. The shaft is topped by the face and ears of a mysterious creature.

DIRECTIONS

The two carved stone crosses are in Bakewell churchyard perched above the centre of the town.

One of two carved crosses in Bakewell church-yard. The shaft is topped by the face and ears of a mysterious creature while the knotwork designs are similar to those on the Hope cross.

Above: *The scene of Christ's crucifix-ion carved on one side of Bradbourne cross. Christ can be clearly seen on the cross with two figures, presumably Roman soldiers, to either side who are piercing him with javelins to test if he is dead.*

Right: *The cross at Bradbourne was only re-erected where it is today after being discovered broken up in a nearby field wall in the nineteenth century. It had probably been destroyed during the Reformation 300 years previously.*

BRADBOURNE CHURCH AND CROSS

Bradbourne was described in Domesday as once belonging to Aelfric who had a church and a priest, along with 12 villagers and 4 smallholders.

The shaft of an Anglo-Viking cross stands in Bradbourne churchyard. The shaft is badly eroded and has had to be put back together from fragments. The east and west faces are decorated with curling vine scrolls that branch off to either side from a central stem. At least three panels depicting human figures can be seen on the north and south faces though they get more badly eroded towards the top. The bottom south-facing panel clearly shows a scene from Christ's crucifixion.

The cross was only erected in the churchyard in 1886 after being found in a nearby field wall. It had been removed and damaged during the Reformation of the sixteenth and early seventeenth centuries, possibly losing its cross at this time. Overlooked and unrecognised for generations, being used as one half of a squeezer stile, it was rediscovered in the late eighteenth century but mistaken for a Roman altar. Only later was it identified as an early medieval Christian way side preaching cross and erected in its current position.

Bradbourne church is mostly a Norman and later medieval building, but fragments of Anglo-Saxon architecture can be seen on the north side of the nave.

The shaft of the preaching cross erected by Saint Betti in the 600s AD now stands in Carsington village green, about 4 kilometres east of Bradbourne. It was moved to its present location from the grounds of nearby Hopton Hall.

EARLY MEDIEVAL PERIOD
1600 years ago – 1000 years ago
400AD – 1066AD

Collapse of the Roman Empire

Anglo-Saxon and Viking social and political influence

Sutton Hoo ship burial

Battle of Hastings and Norman Conquest

DIRECTIONS
The church is 100m to the north of Bradbourne village (SK208527).

WIGBER LOW
See the entry for Wigber Low in Chapter 5.

Further Reading

Barnatt, J. 1990 *The Henges, Stone Circles and Ringcairns of the Peak District.* Sheffield: University of Sheffield.

Barnatt, J. 1999 *Taming the land: Peak District farming and ritual in the Bronze Age.* Derbyshire Archaeological Journal, vol. 119.

Barnatt, J. 2000 *To each their own: Later prehistoric farming communities and their monuments in the Peak.* Derbyshire Archaeological Journal, vol. 120.

Barnatt, J. and Smith, K. 2004 *Peak District: landscapes through time.* Macclesfield: Windgather.

Barnatt, J., Bevan, B. and Edmonds, M. 2002 *Gardom's Edge: a landscape through time.* Antiquity, 76, 50-56.

Bevan, B. 2000 *Peak Practice: what ever happened to the iron age in the southern Pennines?* In Harding, J. and Johnson, R. (eds) *Northern Pasts: interpretations of the later prehistory of northern England and southern Scotland, 141-156.* Oxford: Archaeopress. BAR British Series 302.

Bevan, B. 2004 *The Upper Derwent: 10,000 years in a Peak District valley.* Stroud: Tempus.

Bevan, B. 2005 *Peaks Romana: The Peak District Romano-British rural upland settlement survey 1998-2000,* Derbyshire Archaeological Journal, vol. 125.

Coombs, D.G. and Thompson, H. 1979 *Excavations of the hillfort of Mam Tor, Derbyshire 1965-69.* Derbyshire Archaeological Journal, vol. 99.

Edmonds, M. and Seaborne, T. 2002 *Prehistory In The Peak.* Stroud: Tempus.

Hart, C.R. 1981 *The North Derbyshire Archaeological Survey.* Chesterfield: North Derbyshire Archaeological Trust.

Hodges, R. 2006 *Roystone Grange: 6000 years of a Peakland landscape.* Stroud: Tempus.

Radley, J., and Marshall, G. 1963 *Mesolithic sites in South-west Yorkshire.* Yorkshire Archaeological Journal, vol. 41.

Sidebottom, P. 1999 *Stone crosses of the Peak and the 'sons of Eadwulf'.* Derbyshire Archaeological Journal, vol. 118.

Wroe, P. 1982 *Roman Roads of the Peak District.* Derbyshire Archaeological Journal, vol. 102.

The Derbyshire Archaeological Journal is an annual publication of the Derbyshire Archaeological Society. It contains many articles on the latest archaeological discoveries and projects in the region and can be found in some reference libraries.

Useful Websites

Peak Experience
www.peak-experience.org.uk

Peak District – a living landscape
www.peakdistrict-nationalpark.info/index.html

Dig Sheffield
www.idigsheffield.org.uk

Derbyshire Archaeology Society
www.derbyshireas.org.uk/

Hunter Archaeological Society (Sheffield)
www.shef.ac.uk/archaeology/hunter

Gardom's Edge
www.gardoms-edge.group.shef.ac.uk/index.html

Cresswell Crags
www.creswell-crags.org.uk

Mellor Archaeological Trust
www.mellorarchaeology.org.uk

Poole's Cavern
www.poolescavern.co.uk

Council for British Archaeology
www.britarch.ac.uk

The Modern Antiquarian
www.themodernantiquarian.com

Megalithic Portal
www.megalithic.co.uk

Regional Museums

Weston Park Museum, Sheffield

Weston Park Museum re-opened in 2006 after a multi-million pound refit funded by the Heritage Lottery Fund. Now aimed mainly at children and families, visitors to the museum can explore the past through a series of interactive displays. Prehistoric and Roman artefacts on are display in a small gallery to the sound of running water and other natural sounds. The History Lab has a Sheffield and Peak District timeline and Anglo-Saxon displays. These include New Stone Age and Bronze Age grave goods, including a good range of flint tools, shale necklaces, Beakers, Food Vessels and the large Collared Urns that contained cremations. Many of these are from Bateman's own collection. There are three boulders with rock art and a replica of the Gardom's Edge cup and ring stone. Roman finds include an altar, lead lamp and lead weights from *Navio*. The original Benty Grange helmet and a replica are on show next to contemporary jewellery, weapons and hanging bowl fittings. There is even one of Thomas Bateman's named lead tags that he left in the bottom of his excavations.

A selection of the Museum's objects can be explored online at iDig Sheffield (www.idigsheffield.org.uk). Here you can search through a user-friendly database of photographs by site name, type of object or period. Each photograph is accompanied by a description and links to related images.

Weston Park Museum
Western Bank
Sheffield S10 2TP
0114 278 2600
info@sheffieldgalleries.org.uk
www.sheffieldgalleries.org.uk/coresite/html/WPM.asp

Buxton Museum and Art Gallery

Buxton Museum and Art Gallery is at the heart of the Peak District. The archaeology collections cover the period from the earliest evidence of people in the Peak District (linking closely to the geology collections) to the end of the medieval period.

The Prehistoric collections cover the periods from the Paleolithic through to the Neolithic period, including stone tools from Arbor Low, Kinder Scout and Edale. Some of these tools were found in re-examination of Bateman's excavations of barrows in the Peak. There are also Bronze and Iron age artefacts, including human remains, pottery and tools. The period of Roman occupation is recorded through the excavations at Melandra and Carsington, and significantly Buxton itself. Two significant deposits at Thirst House and Poole's Cavern provide evidence of fine bronze-smithing skills locally during the period of the occupation.

There is also a large collection of Pleistocene mammal bones and fossils.

Buxton Museum and Art Gallery
Terrace Road
Buxton SK17 6DA
01298 24658
buxton.museum@derbyshire.gov.uk
www.derbyshire.gov.uk/leisure/buxton_museum/